Discovering
Medieval Houses
in England and Wales
Anthony Emery

A Shire book

For my nephew, James,
whose enthusiasm for history
might extend to architecture.

British Library Cataloguing in Publication Data: Emery, Anthony. Discovering medieval houses. – (Discovering series; no. 297) 1. Architecture, Domestic – England 2. Architecture, Domestic – Wales 3. Architecture, Medieval – England 4. Architecture, Medieval – Wales 5. Dwellings – England – History – To 1500 6. Dwellings – Wales – History – To 1500 I. Title 728'.0942'0902 ISBN-13: 978 0 7478 0655 4.

Note: To help identify the location of a residence, the relevant county is included when it is first mentioned in the text. Counties are also included in the index.

Front cover: *Great Chalfield Manor, Wiltshire.*
Title page: *The hall at Gainsborough Old Hall, Lincolnshire.*
Back cover: *The hall at Dartington Hall, Devon.*

All photographs and plans are by the author. The illustrations on pages 23 and 24 are from the Bayeux Tapestry, Centre Guillaume le Conquérant, and that of Winchester College on page 151 is by David Loggan (1675). The author is particularly appreciative of the helpful suggestions made by Sarah Pearson FSA and Nicholas Cooper FSA during the preparation of this text.

Published in 2007 by Shire Publications Ltd, Cromwell House, Church Street, Princes Risborough, Buckinghamshire HP27 9AA, UK. (Website: www.shirebooks.co.uk) Copyright © 2007 by Anthony Emery. First published 2007. Number 297 in the Discovering series. ISBN-13: 978 0 7478 0655 4.
Anthony Emery is hereby identified as the author of this work in accordance with Section 77 of the Copyright, Designs and Patents Act, 1988.

Printed in Malta by Gutenberg Press Ltd, Gudja Road, Tarxien PLA 19, Malta.

Contents

Ashleworth Court, Gloucestershire. The plan of central hall with its tall windows, services block in line at the lower end, and projecting cross-wing at the upper end is a classic late medieval plan. Despite the later insertion of a floor in the hall and a number of internal partitions, the basic character of this mid-fifteenth-century house is unimpaired.

1. Introduction

Houses are a reflection of society. They indicate the standing of the builder, the size of his estate, his financial resources and his social status. They reflect the scale of his household and possibly the fluctuating fortunes of his successors. For a house is a living organism. It expresses the needs, the taste, the standing and the imagination of its owner – considerations which were just as important in medieval England as they are today.

The crown, the aristocracy and the gentry were the leaders of medieval society. It is therefore primarily their residences that are examined in the following pages. They were wealthier, could afford high-quality materials, employ craftsmen and be innovative. Their homes are better documented and can therefore be related to the relevant social context. They set the building and furnishing standards to which other people aspired. Yet society fluctuated and broadened, particularly during the later Middle Ages, so that consideration can also be given to merchant, yeoman and peasant houses.

Almost all of the five hundred or so medieval stone castles that survive in England and Wales are ruined, whereas there are nearly twice that number of high-status medieval houses and they are mainly roofed – seventy or so from the twelfth century, about one hundred from the thirteenth century, and over seven hundred from the fourteenth and fifteenth centuries. To this number should be added those of lesser standing, bringing the total to almost 1500 properties, excluding those of merchants and peasants. Of course, they vary in scale and extent. Some are virtually complete, such as Haddon Hall or Ightham Mote. Some exist in part, like Dartington Hall or Herstmonceux Castle. Others

Herstmonceux Castle, Sussex. Built c.1436–49, Herstmonceux is a castle in name only. It is a comfortable residence with a showy defensive gatehouse, built by a knight on a scale that vied with the house of a magnate or even a king.

Herstmonceux Castle. This rear frontage shows more clearly that the castle is a comfortable residence hiding behind a superficially defensive cloak.

retain a single structure – a chamber block (Boothby Pagnell Manor), a gateway (Mackworth), or a chapel (Horne's Place). A number are open to the public, but the continued habitation of the majority means that access can be severely limited or unavailable. This helps to explain why the early development of houses has been less studied than that of castles, where visiting and examination are rarely a problem.

The use of the word 'castle' has long been a source of academic confusion and deliberate obfuscation, particularly insofar as late medieval residences are concerned. It is often forgotten that the upper echelons of medieval society owned and occupied houses as well as castles and that they were far less aware of the differences than present-day architectural students. In any case, the need for fortresses in England and Wales during the Middle Ages, in which military considerations were paramount, had essentially passed by the early fourteenth century. A small number of castles, such as Warwick and Raglan, were subsequently developed with powerful fortifications but the word 'castle', unknown before the sixteenth century, has been indiscriminately ascribed ever since to houses of external defensive show and considerable internal comfort, such as Hever and Herstmonceux. Stokesay was not called a castle until the sixteenth century, Broughton until the nineteenth, and Aydon was given the name only during the twentieth. The original function of a residence that bears the generic name 'castle' therefore needs to be analysed so that a house which is primarily intended for residential occupation, regardless of its external character, can be differentiated from a fortress which had a defensive imperative.

This short study considers a number of key aspects about early domestic residences:

Attribution and ownership. There is a broad range of resources that help us to date a house. They might also indicate who was responsible for its construction and his standing in society.

Architectural development. Nearly all houses include the basic components of hall, chamber and service unit but by the later Middle Ages the majority of properties had become far more complex. Most houses under consideration are therefore a study of accretion and expansion rather than a single-period build, though the latter type are architecturally more important.

Building materials. To what extent do houses reflect the use of traditional and local building materials? Do they contribute as much to its structural development as to its aesthetics?

Contents and furnishings. Few original furnishings have survived so that all recovered evidence is particularly important. Its extent and quality reflected the social standing and lifestyle of the occupants and what they considered necessary to meet their physical, aesthetic and domestic needs.

Political development. Political events rarely affected houses across the whole of England and Wales but they could dramatically change the form and character of those in regions affected by political turbulence such as the north throughout the fourteenth century or the south-east during the Hundred Years' War.

Social development. Architecture is essentially a framework to enclose space. What was that space used for and how did it reflect the changing needs of a household? This develops into an appreciation of how the living patterns of the occupants and the organisation of the household were achieved through the planning function.

Comparable buildings. During the later Middle Ages, communal residences such as academic colleges and colleges of secular canons were influenced by and, in turn, furthered house development.

Town dwellings. To what extent were town houses affected by their immediate environment? Were they modest versions of those of superior status or did they develop independently?

Agrarian society. Do many yeoman and peasant houses survive today? Were they of standard form or subject to regional differences?

This study is an introduction to a broad field that encompasses social and political history, archaeology and archives, as well as architectural and investigative disciplines. None of them is self-contained but their interaction helps us to build up a picture of house development and achievement during the five centuries from 1000 onwards. For houses took on a recognisable form during the twelfth and thirteenth centuries, and they continued to expand and develop – physically, culturally and socially – as a mirror of society through the fourteenth and fifteenth centuries. As a consequence, the first great era of house building in England and Wales was an achievement of the later Middle Ages and not, as is usually asserted, an attainment of the Tudors.

Biddestone, Wiltshire

2. Building records

Given that the purpose of most buildings is immediately obvious, the first two questions that arise about a particular property – whether house, church, castle or abbey – are when was it built and by whom? Sometimes the answers can be stated with confidence; sometimes the answers rely on probability or guesswork, depending on the extent and quality of the relevant material. This chapter describes the range of sources available that help determine the construction date and development phases of a house. As they vary in quality and accuracy, they are described in their order of value.

CONTRACTS AND ACCOUNTS

England and Wales retain the most extensive archive of medieval government in Europe. We therefore have detailed records covering the majority of royal works undertaken from the eleventh century onwards. They have been summarised in the first two volumes of *The History of the King's Works*, edited by H. M. Colvin (1963). They document work undertaken at the royal palaces, castles and houses as well as at crown-supported abbeys, colleges and charitable establishments, sometimes with the names of the craftsmen involved. Because the Duchy of Lancaster came into royal hands after Henry Bolingbroke, Duke of Lancaster, became King Henry IV in 1399, many of the Duchy records have also been preserved, including those for the Savoy Palace (London), Tutbury (Staffordshire), Leicester and Lancaster castles.

Private records are far more sparse and have survived only through good fortune. Even so, a number exist for residences that are still standing and these contribute an element of human interest to their construction. They are essentially of two forms – contracts and building accounts. A contract is an

Portchester Castle, Hampshire. The hall and royal apartments built for Richard II between 1396 and 1399 lay within the outer wall of the Norman castle. The detailed accounts show that candles were used at night to hasten its completion.

Bolton Castle, Yorkshire. Still partially roofed, this major residence not only exhibits an unfettered design of the late fourteenth century but it is an excellent record of the permanent accommodation needed for the home of a leading magnate and his family.

agreement to build a residence to the terms and specification laid down by the owner, such as that between Ralph, Lord Stafford, and the master mason John of Burcestre, on 13th January 1348 for the tower-house on the earlier motte at Stafford Castle. A comparable contract survives for the construction of Bolton Castle in Wensleydale (Yorkshire) dated from 14th September 1378, between Richard, Lord Scrope, and John Lewyn, detailing the form of the east range,

Bolton Castle. An example of a balanced façade, sought in late fourteenth-century houses and their successors. It is interrupted only by the line of second-floor chapel windows.

two eastern towers and the eastern part of the south front. Its terms suggest that work had already begun, though the royal licence giving permission for the castle to be crowned with battlements was not granted until a year later. The existing structure, as well as John Leland's comment that the castle took eighteen years to build, shows that there must have been a further contract that no longer survives covering the remainder of the residence.

The building accounts that have survived are usually the summary sheets prepared for audit purposes rather than the detailed weekly sheets for pay and essential items of expenditure. They include the records for some of the colleges at Oxford and Cambridge as well as several private enterprises, including five building statements covering work undertaken for Ralph, Lord Cromwell, at Tattershall Castle (Lincolnshire) between 1434 and 1446. Lord Cromwell was a highly efficient Treasurer of England, who personally checked his domestic records, while the precise fourteen-month account for his manor house at Wingfield (Derbyshire) from November 1442 to December 1443 has proved critical in helping to establish the date and building sequence of this important Derbyshire mansion.

The most detailed building accounts are those for rebuilding the family seat of Lord Hastings at Kirby Muxloe (Leicestershire), recording all activities week

Kirby Muxloe Castle, Leicestershire: gatehouse and west tower. John Cowper, the master mason responsible for Tattershall church, was at the same time working on this fortified house for Lord Hastings. Brick was used here, in contrast with the stone chosen for Hastings's castle at Ashby de la Zouch, just as Lord Cromwell had used brick at Tattershall Castle but local stone at Wingfield Manor.

by week between October 1480 and December 1484. They confirm that most work occurred each year between early May and the end of October, though some preliminary work had taken place during the winter of 1480, when the earlier hall and family apartments were repaired, trees round the site were cut down, and the ditchers started to excavate the moat. Masons began laying the wall footings in May 1481 with brick made locally and stone brought from a few miles to the north. At the end of the season unfinished walls were covered with straw and bracken to protect them from frost, and most of the craftsmen and labourers were laid off, except for a few retained at one penny a day less than in the summer. Work progressed so quickly that some of the towers were finished by October 1482 and continued through the following winter to enable the gatehouse to be completed. The floors were inserted and the angle towers were roofed with lead but, in June 1483, Lord Hastings was suddenly arrested and executed by a suspicious Richard III. The accounts show that work stopped immediately for three months and was resumed only on a much reduced scale to allow Lady Hastings to occupy the structures completed so far. The outlay totalled £330 3s 0d (1481), £397 5s 8½d (1482) and £205 8s 6½d (to June 1483), with Lady Hastings incurring a further £61 0s 4d to December 1484.

LICENCES TO CRENELLATE

Although only a modest number of building contracts and accounts have survived, more than 590 licences giving permission to crown a property with battlements were issued between 1200 and 1550, with a handful thereafter to 1622. The granting of these licences was a royal prerogative awarded to a petitioner who sought (and paid for) the privilege. The only exceptions to the 577 crown grants were the fourteen further licences awarded in the three regions where royal jurisdiction was limited – the Palatinates of Durham and Chester and the Duchy of Lancaster after 1351. Because of renewals and repeats, the number of individual properties covered by all these licences was about 520. More than 80 per cent were issued for private residences held by lay and ecclesiastical magnates, knights and gentry, with the remainder shared almost equally between those responsible for monastic precincts, town houses and town walls.

Embattlement licences were not granted to regulate fractious barons or to reward favoured courtiers but were a practice that conferred status on the house owner while adding modestly to Treasury funds. Licences were not initiated by the crown but requested by supplicants as a structural mark of distinction. They were proof that authority had been given for the external evidence of social standing that embattlement proclaimed.

The earliest licences in England were granted by King John in 1200 but the majority were concentrated in the years between 1250 and about 1410, with the high point reached during the first half of Edward III's reign, 1330 to 1350. Where a licence can be tested against other documentary evidence or structure, the earliest seem to apply to castles where fortification was the dominant characteristic, but they came to apply to fortified manor houses (Weoley, Birmingham, 1264; Acton Burnell, Shropshire, 1284) and then to encompass a broad span of houses of increasingly domestic character (Woodsford, Dorset, 1335; Great Dixter, Sussex, 1479). Their purpose and practice over four centuries have been the cause of much confusion to architectural students, compounded by the lack of logic in their award or distribution. No licence

Woodsford 'Castle', Dorset. Though a licence to crenellate was granted in 1335 to William Whitfield for his house at Woodsford, architectural detailing shows that this residential range is at least a generation later. In 1367 Whitfield sold the manor to Sir Guy Brian (died 1390), who was responsible for this range, which formed a multi-unitary complex to a now lost hall and quadrangular house. The thatched roof is a mid-seventeenth-century replacement of the original tiles.

exists for the tower-house added at Warkworth Castle (Northumberland) during the 1390s or the contemporary development of Wressle Castle (Yorkshire) by the Earl of Northumberland and his brother respectively, but they were obtained by their neighbour, Lord Neville, for his prominent castles at Raby (County Durham) and Sheriff Hutton (Yorkshire). Licences were sought by all who aspired to the upper ranks of society, irrespective of the size of the property, so that they embraced major residences such as Hampton Court, Leominster (Herefordshire, 1434) and modest houses like Woodmanton (Worcestershire, 1332) and Rye House (Hertfordshire, 1447).

A number of licences still survive among a house's archives (Chillingham Castle, Northumberland, 1344; Oxburgh Hall, Norfolk, 1482) but the principal source for their existence is enrolment by the royal chancery, principally on the Patent Rolls but with a few detailed on the Close Rolls and the Inquisitions Post Mortem. Researched and listed by Charles Coulson, they are an invaluable indication of construction, giving us a relatively clear idea of the year when building was planned or taking place. Thus the licence awarded to Sir John Devereux in 1392 for Penshurst Place (Kent) relates to the towered enclosure surrounding the earlier house built by Sir John Pulteney under licence in 1341. They bring an element of precision to many houses for which we otherwise have no documentary evidence (Yate Court, Gloucestershire, 1299; Rotherfield Greys, Oxfordshire, 1346), for it is no coincidence that licensing became more frequent with the development of stone-built houses. Yet licences need to be treated with caution. That for Kirby Muxloe was granted in 1474 although the building accounts show that construction did not begin until six years later. The gap between erection and licensing at Bolton Castle has already been mentioned,

Spofforth Castle, Yorkshire. A manor house developed by Henry, Lord Percy, under a licence to crenellate issued in 1308. The hall, seen from the courtyard, is apparently a ground-floor apartment, updated during the fifteenth century.

while Richard, Duke of York, set his men to work on building Hunsdon House (Hertfordshire) in March 1446, fourteen months before he obtained permission to crenellate the property. Occasionally an owner sought a pardon for embattling without authority, as occurred at Ragley (Warwickshire, 1381), Farleigh Hungerford (Somerset, 1383), and Sudeley Castle (Gloucestershire, 1458), thereby helping us to identify a *terminus post quem* for their construction.

DENDROCHRONOLOGY

Any analysis of a building depends on detailed plans, carefully drawn elevations and cross-sections. These long-established practices have been

Spofforth Castle. The hall and residential block were built on falling ground, allowing undercrofts to be developed beneath both structures. They followed the same plan as the rooms above but the hall, shown here, was rebuilt during the fifteenth century.

joined by modern technical advances such as rectified photography and photogrammetry. They are particularly useful for the precise analysis of the composition of stone walling, such as the apparently uniform outer wall of the great hall at Laugharne Castle (Carmarthenshire). Such techniques have helped to show that this late thirteenth-century structure was subject to a mid-fourteenth-century extension and renewed hall floor, two phases of late sixteenth-century insertions and considerable repair work in the eighteenth or nineteenth century.

The most significant advance, however, has been a consequence of dendrochronology, the analysis of tree rings in timberwork. A tree trunk or branch adds a new ring of growth each year, though the annual rate of growth varies according to climatic conditions. Careful study and comparison of the tree-ring growth of many timbers has enabled a master pattern to be created stretching back more than a thousand years. Samples from timbers to be dated can be matched against this. Some trees, such as oak (the primary resource in medieval England and Wales), provide a clearer pattern than others, such as beech or ash. The more sapwood present in the sample, the more precisely the felling period can be dated, though only the existence of the bark at the outer edge can give a firm date for the last year of tree growth before felling. Usually a little time elapses between felling a tree and its use in construction (up to about three years) but dendrochronology gives a date when the timber was cut down. The consequence is that not only has our appreciation of house construction been radically altered through the analysis of the roof timbers, but whole areas of study, such as that of timber houses in Kent, have been totally reappraised. The hall and solar blocks at Ightham Mote in that county, formerly

Ightham Mote, Kent. The hall and solar blocks from the courtyard illustrate the contemporary combination of stone and timber framing – a practice followed throughout this house's development.

14

attributed to the early fourteenth and sixteenth centuries respectively, have now been shown to have been developed in sequence with timbers felled in 1330 (solar 1), 1331 (solar 2), 1337 (hall) and 1342 (adjacent chapel block). The university laboratories at Oxford, Sheffield, Nottingham, Lampeter and London provide data which is published annually in the volumes of *Vernacular Architecture*. It is here that the majority of architectural historians are alerted to reassessments such as that for the hall at Baguley Hall, Manchester. Confidently attributed after detailed study in 1989 to the second quarter of the fourteenth century, dendrochronology thirteen years later revealed that the structure was erected in 1398–9, with further research showing that it was designed for dual rather than single family occupancy (page 75). This analysis has necessitated the house's reappraisal as a key building in the development of timber-framing in north-west England.

SUPPLEMENTARY SOURCES

The range of written sources mentioning building activity extends from licences to recruit staff to the notebooks of post-medieval travellers. Robert Skillyngton, the mason at Kenilworth Castle (Warwickshire), was granted a licence to impress craftsmen and labourers in July 1391 for work at the castle, though the buildings demanding attention were not specified. Wills occasionally help by mentioning bequests to complete construction work already in hand, such as that made by Sir John Noreys in 1465 for the completion of Ockwells Manor (Berkshire). Permission given to the Earl of Huntingdon to use slate from a quarry owned by Exeter Cathedral for his Devon manor house helps to pinpoint the development of Dartington Hall to the years close to 1388.

The comments of late medieval travellers include those by William Worcester and John Leland, who brought a degree of accurate reporting on individual buildings that warrants serious consideration. Worcester, the first topographer of England, was secretary to Sir John Fastolf of Caister Castle (Norfolk) from about 1438 until Fastolf's death in 1459. He coped with the administration (and litigation) of his patron's estates for the next ten years and concluded life in genteel clerical poverty. Blind in one eye, he made three pilgrimages in his old age – to St Michael's Mount (1478), Walsingham (1479) and Glastonbury (1480) – keeping detailed notes of his itineraries, recording the buildings that he saw, and commenting on standing and subsequently lost buildings (Sheen Palace, Surrey; Rey Manor, Norfolk; Hunsdon House), magnate households (Thomas Beaufort, Duke of Exeter) and unusual sights (Wookey Hole). His notes serve as a judicious prelude to the vastly more detailed and extended journeys made by John Leland between 1539 and 1545. Leland was a polymath who received his royal commission to search for English antiquities and peruse monastic libraries for manuscripts of value in 1533. His five journeys were not measured topographical surveys across the country, for East Anglia was barely covered, while there are only scattered notes for south-east England. Yet he was an insatiable researcher and accurate observer of subjects ranging from archaeological sites to newly built houses, local industries and folklore. His architectural comments, often fleshed out with details from his gentrified and aristocratic hosts, are our guide to the state of countless residences of late medieval England and Wales before they were modified, extended or pulled down, as with Wickham Court (Kent), Stourton House (Wiltshire) and Wressle

Castle. Though his comments were often brief, he was a careful recorder, sometimes doubting the veracity of his informants, and a peerless eye-witness to the transitional years between late medieval and early modern England.

BUILDING ASCRIPTIONS

Building records of a different character are the occasional inscriptions and coats of arms that have survived. Inscriptions from the late fourteenth century include the foundation stones incised 'Thomas' and 'Alianore' on the postern tower and the footings of a nearby structure at Caldicot Castle (Monmouthshire), supporting the documentary evidence for a major building programme in 1383–8 by Thomas, Duke of Gloucester, and his wife, Eleanor de Bohun. The portraits in glass in the east window of Winchester College

Thornbury Castle, Gloucestershire. One of the finest early Tudor palaces. The inscription above the principal entrance states that it was begun in 1511 by Edward, third Duke of Buckingham. The martial frontage terminates in the south-west tower, the only one completed before Buckingham's execution in 1521.

chapel identify and depict the responsible master mason, carpenter, glazier and clerk of works.

Coats of arms in stone, wood or glass are not infrequent but need to be treated with care as they may not be in a contemporary structural context. The arms of Thomas Palmer (died 1475) and his second wife, whom he married before 1457, support the architectural character of the porch and bay window added to the earlier but otherwise plain gentry hall at Nevill Holt (Leicestershire). The highly important armorial glass in the windows of the hall at Ockwells Manor limit that apartment's construction to between 1451 and 1459, while the name and badge of William Grafton help to identify his responsibility for the otherwise undocumented rebuilding of the hall and residential block at Buckland Old Rectory (Gloucestershire) during Edward IV's reign. The west of England is particularly rich in heraldic displays identifying building responsibility, including Athelhampton Hall (Dorset), Bradley Manor (Devon), Croscombe Hall (Somerset), Fiddleford Manor (Dorset), Great Chalfield Manor (Wiltshire) and Thornbury Castle (Gloucestershire).

EXCAVATION

Excavation usually destroys. A satisfactory result depends on accurate recording as well as on the detailed study of deposits and artefacts, particularly the stratigraphic relationship of accumulated deposits and their chronological relationship. This helps to identify the sequential development of the site. Where a site has been abandoned, then excavation is probably the most valuable way of determining its history. Where part of the site is still occupied, it is a valuable addition to its understanding. Few sites can be excavated below an occupied building, but this can bring valuable results, as at Hunsdon House,

Weoley Castle, West Midlands. The fortified house of\a middle-ranking family, 3 miles from central Birmingham. The late thirteenth-century walls and towers round an irregular court were excavated between the 1930s and 1950s.

where the basement revealed the foundations of the massive brick tower-house built by Richard, Duke of York, in 1445–8. There is much merit in only partially excavating a site, as occurred with the second court at Dartington Hall (Devon) in 1962, so that a later generation with more sophisticated techniques might be able to settle the unresolved interpretations of this site. What is not acceptable is the excavation of a property and the failure, for whatever reason, to write up the results. Examples are invidious to identify but they extend to a number of major sites, with the consequence that future researchers lack the basic information for checking or re-interpreting the earlier excavated evidence.

STRUCTURAL SURVEY

Where there is no documentary or other reliable dating evidence, a structural survey of a house can point to its likely development. This involves examining each part in turn, looking for evidence of earlier or later building phases or alterations to the original fabric. These can be traced through changes in materials and roof lines as well as by noting wall joints and decorative detailing. This work is necessarily imprecise but it usually allows the house's development to be traced within a range of twenty to fifty years. This is the most usual method for determining the age of a house and has not yet been superseded as the way of assessing the development even of leading properties such as Sudeley Castle, Haddon Hall (Derbyshire) and Penshurst Place.

Sudeley Castle, Gloucestershire. A spectacular mid-fifteenth-century double-courtyard mansion. The detached chapel stands on the right. A lodging range of the outer court is now marked by the line of late Tudor windows, while the second court (left) holds the ruined apartments of Richard, Duke of Gloucester.

COMPARATIVE BUILDING ANALYSIS

In the absence of any documentary, scientific or archaeological evidence, it is possible to indicate a house's likely period of construction by comparison with nearby buildings of known construction date. The parameters will necessarily be broad, but they can be helpful in identifying likely responsibility for development or extension. The two-storeyed entrance range of Brinsop Court in Herefordshire can be attributed to the period 1310–20, based on pairs of cusped lights with well-shaped labels, similar to those lighting the crypt below the chancel of nearby Madley church of *c*.1315–20, for which offerings for its construction were made in 1318. The spectacular guild hall of St Mary in Coventry of the 1390s was based on that built by John of Gaunt twenty years earlier at Kenilworth Castle. It not only followed the precedent of first-floor construction above an earlier undercroft but adopted the same four-centred window and doorway form, extended stair and lobby approach, high table oriel window and embattled parapet (since replaced). The detached chapel erected by

Warkworth Castle, Northumberland. The construction of this tower-house has been attributed to an impossibly wide range of dates between the later fourteenth and early sixteenth centuries. There are no building accounts, licence or documentary references, but a comparison with other dated buildings in the area makes it fairly certain that this symmetrical but complex structure was erected between 1390 and 1400 by the first Duke of Northumberland.

Meare Manor Farm, Somerset. A manor house of the abbots of Glastonbury, Meare Manor has long been a working farm and was built by Abbot Sodbury (1334–42). Continuous occupation has not devalued the early character of this essentially single-period house, but, like many medieval houses, it warrants further research and analysis. Its original internal layout is unclear, particularly the position of the kitchen, while the principal rooms on the upper floor may have been served by a lost ground-floor hall. The purpose of the so-called 'chapel' with its now blocked windows is contradicted by the contemporary chimney stack and fireplace (enlarged in the fifteenth century), while the property also needs to be considered in the wider context of its immediate watery landscape.

Ralph, Baron Boteler, at Sudeley Castle is considerably richer in its detailing than the remainder of his double courtyard mansion of 1441–58, for the chapel closely resembles the contemporary aisles of Winchcombe parish church, which Boteler supported financially during the early 1460s.

We shall now consider the key stages in the architectural development of a house from the eleventh to the sixteenth centuries, bearing in mind that these essentially occur in those of high status – the crown, the baronage and the gentry – with a trickle-down effect to those of lesser standing. They may have made up less than 0.1 per cent of the population but their power and influence were overwhelming and their homes reflect this throughout the Middle Ages.

3. Architectural developments: 500-1300

ANGLO-SAXON RESIDENCES

The earliest standing houses in England and Wales were built in the decades following the Norman Conquest, the majority of them during the twelfth century. Pre-Conquest evidence is limited to archaeological, literary and documentary sources but covers a broad range, extending from residences of royal or high status to vernacular town houses and shops. Royal palaces have been excavated at Yeavering for early Northumbrian kings, at Northampton for middle Saxon kings, and at Cheddar (Somerset) for the kings of Wessex. The palace of Yeavering consisted of several buildings that reached a peak under kings Aethelfrith and Edwin (592–632), when the residence included a 120 feet (37 metres) long hall, a smaller hall, an assembly area – all in line – and possibly a chapel, all within a palisaded enclosure. These structures were in wood with the principal hall, aisled and buttressed. There were a central hearth, walls lined with planks, and an inner room. The royal palace at Cheddar was established in the ninth century, repeating the form of a narrow 120 feet long hall with a chamber and other subsidiary buildings, enclosed by a ditch. A second broader hall and detached chamber were added in the tenth century, and an imposing third one, with massive timber posts creating aisles to the body of the hall, during the early twelfth century. The outlines of these buildings have been marked on the ground of the 1960s school that now covers part of the site. The shorter-lived palace at Northampton also showed a succession of high-status halls, the earlier of timber (mid eighth century) and the later of stone (early ninth century), abandoned a century later. All three sites highlight the popularity of the hall as the key structure of English domestic architecture from

Cheddar Palace, Somerset: excavated site.

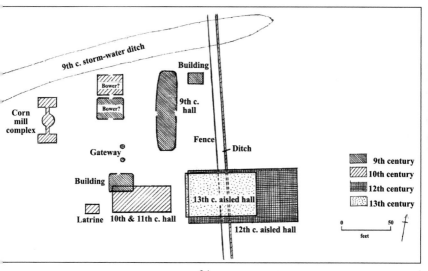

21

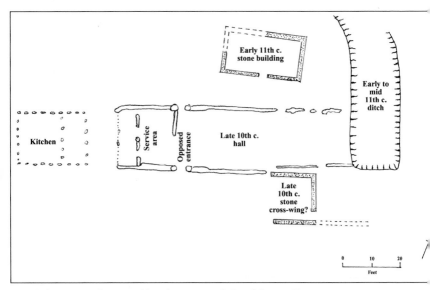

Sulgrave, Northamptonshire: the excavated site of the pre-Conquest manor.

the earliest time, and the practice of separate structures for associated functions.

Early manor houses have been excavated at Goltho in Lincolnshire and at Sulgrave in Northamptonshire. The excavations at Goltho revealed a number of structures rebuilt and moved between the late tenth century and the early twelfth, including the replacement in *c.*1000 of two earlier halls by one with a single aisle, central hearth and partitioned end chamber, as well as a kitchen, a ladies' bower, and possibly a weaving shed. The excavation of the high-status late tenth-century site at Sulgrave revealed what has been interpreted as an unaisled ground-floor hall, 55 feet by 18 feet (16.7 by 5.5 metres), with opposing entrances, a bench down one side wall, a screened service area at the lower end with a putative detached kitchen beyond. At the upper end of this timber-built hall was a stone structure, thought to have been a more private cross-wing, but this interpretation of what became the standard medieval house plan is very tentative. The buildings of each site were surrounded by a ditch and fenced enclosure known as a ringwork. The approach to such lordly residences was marked by an entrance tower or *burh-geat*. Its purpose was to make a statement of rank and serve a quasi-ceremonial function rather than be a defensive structure.

The excavations at Goltho and Sulgrave have shown that these late Saxon residences were taken over by the first wave of Norman invaders during the late eleventh century and altered to serve as castles. This practice has also been identified at a number of other sites, such as Eynsford (Kent) and Castle Acre (Norfolk). Not surprisingly, the Norman earthworks and associated stone buildings have attracted most attention, but the excavations showed that more late Saxon high-status houses are likely to have survived than previously thought through their adoption as early Norman castles. This promises to be a rewarding field for study and excavation.

From the first, the hall was the principal apartment of any residence between the sixth and sixteenth centuries, but its function was not unchanging. Until the fourteenth century it was the roofed area where all the household gathered for meals, where business was carried out, justice was administered, and entertainment and communality took place. Yet, from earliest times, documentary and archaeological evidence shows that owners of standing and their families were able to withdraw to a more private room or *camera* so that the earliest residences were usually two-roomed or, more precisely, hall and chamber structures. Nearby would be the roofed units necessary for the associated domestic function of kitchen, stables and workshops, irregularly positioned within an enclosure.

Five representations of early English halls and high-status chambers are depicted in the 230 feet (70 metres) long Bayeux Tapestry, usually dated to *c*.1070–80. In these near-contemporary representations, perspective and proportions are distorted to emphasise the interior events being played out inside the buildings. Scene 30 shows an enthroned Edward the Confessor in the ground-floor hall of his palace at Westminster, next to a realistic depiction of his newly completed abbey. It is possible that this same hall (with the enthroned king) is illustrated from a different angle in the first scene of the tapestry, with a two-storey chamber block on one side of the hall (possibly with a first-floor balcony) and a stair turret on the other side. The chamber block is shown in cross-section in the representation of the Confessor's death (scene 32) on a curtain-draped bed in his private upper chamber, with his body being laid out on a mattress in the room below. A more cheerful depiction of a two-storey chamber block in use appears in scene 3, where Harold feasts in the upper room of his house at Bosham (Sussex), approached by an external stair and above a

Bayeux Tapestry, c.1070–80. (Scene 1) Edward the Confessor sits in a chair of state in the hall of his palace at Westminster. The hall is flanked by a turret and a tower, the latter possibly tile-covered.

Bayeux Tapestry, c.1070–80. (Scene 3) King Harold feasting in his house at Bosham, Sussex. This is probably a chamber block with the principal room on the upper floor above a vaulted undercroft. The chamber is approached by an external stair.

pillared lower chamber. The Bayeux Tapestry also shows that the large hall used by King Harold after his enthronement (scene 34) had painted pillars, a decoratively carved roof, animal ridge tiles and pinnacled roof turrets on the storeyed chamber block.

ANGLO-NORMAN HOUSES

Though stone had been the chosen material for late Anglo-Saxon cathedrals and abbey churches, houses prior to the Norman Conquest were almost entirely timber-built. This changed dramatically in the century after the Conquest of 1066, with an enormous surge in stone building, not only for the larger replacement cathedrals and monastic buildings but for many royal and private fortresses and the houses of the more wealthy. By 1200 quarrying had become a major industry, so much so that the sheer volume of construction must have turned the land into a vast building site affecting town and country. High-quality stone was transported great distances, castles and palaces were raised, cathedrals, abbeys and churches were rebuilt, houses and towns were developed, while the choice of this material also began to percolate down the social scale.

Anglo-Norman houses can be divided into two groups: those centred on large ground-floor halls, favoured by the crown, bishops and nobles, and the smaller two-storey stone blocks which are often claimed as self-contained manor houses with first-floor halls, adopted by those of lesser status.

Ground-floor halls

Only a small number of secular Norman halls have survived and they are partial or fragmentary except for one in central England. They are all ground-floor apartments, open to the roof, with a central hearth allowing the smoke to escape through a roof vent or louvre. The entrance was at one end and the high table at the other, sometimes enhanced by wall arcading (later by wall hangings) or larger windows. This was probably the usual form but, from the first years after the Conquest, there was a major variant which lasted for at least two centuries. As the halls of powerful magnates and bishops had to accommodate large numbers of people, the aisled form of construction was usually adopted to achieve the necessary scale. The maximum length of a single roof beam resting on two outer walls was about 35 feet (10.7 metres), so that halls needing a greater width could be achieved only by positioning such massive beams on a line of internal posts or columns from which further beams extended to the outer walls. To achieve grandeur and harmony, the form was usually adopted of two narrow aisles flanking a taller central nave (rather than a single broad aisle), with the aisles covered by lean-to roofs. Furthermore, as these halls were intended to display the status and power of the occupant, they were more elaborately decorated than those of modest households, with the decoration applied to the columns, the aisle arcades and the roof as well as to the windows and doorways.

One of the earliest aisled halls is that built in 1097–9 by William II at the Palace of Westminster. Stone-built on a monumental scale, 240 feet (73.2 metres) long by 67^1/$_2$ feet (20.1 metres) wide, it was intended to impress and overawe his newly conquered subjects at the great feasts and crown-wearing ceremonies held there. The walls were subsequently encased and heightened and the structure re-roofed without aisles by Richard II in the late fourteenth century, but evidence of its early end-wall approach, high-set Norman windows with flanking arcade, and original open wall passage can still be traced.

During the 1960s the foundations were exposed of the large aisled hall with private end chambers at Wolvesey Palace in Winchester built during the 1130s by Henry of Blois, the extremely wealthy Bishop of Winchester. This complex site shows a sequence of development on a royal scale by this most mighty magnate before his death in 1171. By that time, the palace consisted of four extended ranges holding at least thirty-eight ground-floor rooms round a central courtyard. This site should be compared with the royal palace developed at Clarendon, near Salisbury, by Henry II and less satisfactorily excavated during the 1930s. His work included an aisled hall, of which one gable end still stands, and the lower walls of the great wine cellar. Contemporary aristocratic halls survive within Leicester and Oakham (Rutland) castles and episcopal halls at Hereford Palace, Farnham Castle (Surrey) and Old Sarum (Wiltshire, foundations only). All these halls have been attributed to the second half of the twelfth century, suggesting a period of architecturally ambitious development, though Old Sarum might be earlier.

The hall at Oakham, the only standing element of this fortified house, is virtually complete through its continuing use as a court room. The entrance, formerly at the low end, opens into one of the aisles flanking the body of the hall. It is a most stylish apartment with polychrome masonry and stone roof finials externally, and the nave and two aisles well lit internally by two-light windows in both side walls. The massive aisle columns, spanned by dog-tooth decorated arcades, have beautifully carved capitals of animals, birds and

Oakham Castle, Rutland. The hall of this fortified manor house is the finest example of Norman domestic architecture in England. It stands within a large enclosure with other buildings marked by grass-covered mounds. The window at the lower end (right) and the central entrance were interchanged between 1730 and 1847.

musicians by masons who had just finished working at Canterbury Cathedral. This figure sculpture dates the hall to *c*.1180–90. Two doorways in the lower end wall led to the lost service rooms with chamber over, and one at the upper end to the destroyed private apartments of the builder, Walkelin Ferrers.

The remaining aisled halls are also roofed but were timber-built, subsequently encased and divided by

Oakham Castle. The arcade capitals of simple curved leaves are similar to those in the choir of Canterbury Cathedral (1175–84). The two hundred or more horseshoes on the walls bear the names and dates of peers and royalty who have paid this unique due to the lord of the manor of Oakham.

later generations – domestic at Hereford and Farnham, judicial at Leicester. The Hereford structure of *c*.1180 has been studied in more detail than the others and has been shown to be timber-aisled with the tall body of the hall lit by clerestory windows (as at Leicester) with a three-storey chamber block at one end. The bishop's personal accommodation was in a linked block opposite the contemporary entry porch to the hall. Hereford, like Oakham, marks a stage in the movement towards bringing together some of the prime domestic elements under a common roof instead of being separate units as at Cheddar. In these examples, it was the hall and chamber block with proto services, for the private apartments were still kept separate, as occurred similarly at Leicester and Wolvesey. Though utilitarian, early barns such as those at Great Coxwell (Oxfordshire) or Coggeshall (Essex) are the most visible examples today of unencumbered aisled structures of comparable scale and void.

The evidence for more modest houses no longer relies solely on excavated evidence but includes structures identified within later casings. The excavations at Cheddar and the manorial complex at Goltho span the late Saxon and post-Conquest periods, with the buildings being replaced at frequent intervals, seemingly of vernacular character and modest in construction. There has been disagreement over the dating of the different building phases at these sites. Both of them revealed eleventh-century aisled halls but the difference in social status

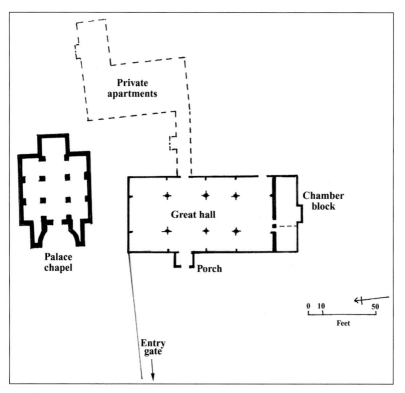

Hereford: ground plan of the Anglo-Norman Bishop's Palace.

Caen Castle, France. This unaisled reception hall built for Henry I is the only standing part of the ducal palace, later developed into Caen Castle. The hall with its gable-end entry was restored in 1960, when the bomb-damaged roof was replaced. The kitchen wing with its exposed chimney was added on the south side in the fourteenth century.

and the uncertainty as to their periods of construction (and reconstruction) make it necessary to exercise caution in postulating any direct link between pre-Conquest aisled halls and their primacy from the later twelfth century.

Several standing buildings have been identified incorporating timber-framed aisled halls erected between 1165 and 1230 (John Walker, *Vernacular Architecture*, 1999). Spanning a broad band across central England from Essex to the Welsh border, they include three manor houses and three houses below manorial status. They are all of box-frame construction, originally with finely detailed halls of two-bay length, and were joined to a further room beyond at least one end. The two Essex houses, Fyfield Hall (1167–85) and Harlowbury near Harlow (1220–5), retain substantial evidence of their original hall roofs. Furthermore, the three aisled houses below manorial status were well enough built to survive to the present day, pointing to future developments in our appreciation of lower-status dwellings.

The inclusion of the word 'aisle' indicates that some halls were small enough not to require them. By far the most splendid example is that built in *c.*1110–20 within Caen Castle in Normandy by Henry I in his role as Duke of Normandy. Like Westminster Hall, this buttressed ducal hall is approached by a fine central door in the lower gable end, opening into a spacious apartment 99 by 36 feet (30.2 by 11.0 metres). It is lit by six round-headed windows in the upper half of both side walls (and one above the entry door), rising above a decorative string course that extends round all sides of the hall. All the windows are internally decorated with colonnettes, but the windows at the upper end are positioned closer together to give more light to the ducal throne on the dais.

The model for this English-influenced hall has not survived, while its successors are a little later, more modest and much altered. Horton Court in Gloucestershire of *c.*1140–50 is the prime example, together with Minster Court, Thanet (Kent, *c.*1120). The former was the principal feature of a rectory while the latter was a grange of St Augustine's Abbey, Canterbury. Horton retains its original form of a 31 feet (9.4 metres) long hall open to the (later) roof with well-preserved Norman features, two chevron-decorated doorways near the lower end and two deeply splayed windows in the north side wall. The two opposing entrances suggest a very early example of a cross-passage, possibly screened, as a vertical timber is still embedded close to one of the doors.

Two-storey chamber blocks

More than twenty-two storeyed stone blocks survive from the Anglo-Norman period, extending from Burton Agnes in Yorkshire to Portslade in Sussex. It used to be thought that these were complete houses with the ground floor used for storage or servants and the upper floor as family accommodation, divided by a partition into a larger outer chamber (the hall) and smaller inner room (the retiring room). The paradigm for this interpretation was Boothby Pagnell Manor House in Lincolnshire. Generally agreed to date from about 1190–1200, this stone building, 56 $1/2$ by 25 $1/2$ feet (17 by 7.5 metres) externally, is divided into a greater and a smaller room at both levels, with the two ground-floor rooms vaulted and the principal upper room reached by a replacement external stair to a Norman doorway. This first-floor 'hall' retains two original round-arched windows, stone-hooded fireplace, chimney stack and doorway to the

Boothby Pagnell Manor House, Lincolnshire. This stand-alone structure was not an entire house but the chamber block of a late Norman complex which included a ground-floor hall. In this instance, a resistivity survey and excavation have indicated that the hall was masonry-built rather than timber-framed. The first-floor four-light window is a replacement of c.1500.

inner room, but there was no internal stair between the two floors. However, the belief that this was a stand-alone building with the hall on the upper floor for defensive purposes is no longer accepted.

John Blair suggested in 1993 that the stone block was not independent but could function sensibly only if it operated in tandem with a ground-floor hall that has not survived. Often of wood and therefore lost, the hall would have been the functional centre of the house with access at its upper or high-status end to the private chambers of the owner. A subsequent resistivity survey in the garden at Boothby Pagnell detected a large rectangular outline, which excavation has shown belonged to a massive early medieval building with stone footings – almost certainly the missing hall with masonry rather than timber walls. The whole area was moat-surrounded for security purposes, but the perception of siting the 'hall' at first-floor level for potential defensive purposes is now seen to be an erroneous twentieth-century explanation influenced by contemporary castle studies.

From this base, one can look backwards and forwards to other similar structures. Research in Normandy has identified a number of sites with aisled halls attached to chamber blocks, as at Bricquebec Castle and Beaumont-le-Richard, but as the form occurred in late Anglo-Saxon England and not in pre-twelfth-century Normandy it seems that the concept was of English origin, exported back to the homeland of the conquerors. Only research or excavation will reveal the hall evidence in the earliest English survivals, which include the still-occupied chamber block of c.1150 at Hemingford Grey Manor House in Cambridgeshire. The first-floor entrance is in the short south gable wall but the opposite gable-end was rebuilt and extended in the eighteenth century when an adjacent building of thirteenth-century date, presumed to be the hall, still stood. This house retains several Norman two-light windows and a wall fireplace, but no original evidence of an internal stair or a division at either level.

Burton Agnes Old Hall in Yorkshire of c.1170–80 is not unlike Boothby Pagnell in possessing a vaulted ground-floor chamber but instead of any internal divisions there was a single room on each floor, linked by an internal stair. This structure was brick-faced by the early eighteenth century, when it became a laundry, destroying any evidence of an attached hall, but it makes more functional sense for it to have been linked to a hall, probably of timber rather than stone, than it would as an independent unit. Cogges Manor Farm in Oxfordshire, Saltford Manor in Somerset, Hatfield Manor House in Yorkshire and Merton Hall in Cambridge are similar late twelfth-century examples, with the larger Merton Hall enjoying a short extension that may have been a garderobe or lavatory block.

This reinterpretation of surviving chamber blocks prior to 1200 has simplified the evolution of the English house propounded by Margaret Wood in *The English Medieval House* (1965) and Michael Thompson in *The Medieval Hall* (1995), for most of the units they considered to be first-floor hall houses were not so designed but were domestic units dependent on halls that were functionally and structurally distinct. The latter were usually of wood and therefore have not survived or have been subsequently replaced. That is not to say there were no first-floor halls, but the small number in central and southern England raised above low-vaulted undercrofts over the five centuries following the Norman Conquest were so purposed for protection or greater status (or

Burton Agnes Manor House, Yorkshire. The vaulted ground-floor chamber of 1170–80 is divided by a row of cylindrical piers into two aisles. The entry is at the lower end, with a spiral stair to the first-floor chamber at the opposite end.

Burton Agnes Manor House. The first-floor chamber, entered from the corner (left), became a laundry in the eighteenth century, blocking the twelfth-century windows. The walls were heightened in the fifteenth century when the present roof was added.

both). They were limited mainly to major castles, headed by the large room (ceremonial rather than domestic) possibly built by the crown in the 1080s at Chepstow Castle (Monmouthshire), converted into a more standard but richly decorated hall and chamber during the 1230s. The more conventional first-floor hall and private chamber above a lesser hall for retainers at Richmond Castle (1071–86) in Yorkshire was a precursor of the grand halls of the thirteenth century (Corfe Castle in Dorset and Ludlow Castle in Shropshire) and those of the fourteenth century at Windsor Castle (Berkshire), Kenilworth Castle (Warwickshire), and Portchester Castle (Hampshire). Status-raised halls were otherwise limited to residences of the highest-ranking owners such as Bishop Jocelyn at Wells Palace (Somerset, 1230s), Bishop Gower at St David's Palace (Pembrokeshire, 1330s), and Bishop Wykeham's academic colleges at Oxford and Winchester (1380s). It occasionally involved a wealthy monastery such as Cleeve Abbey (Somerset, c.1440–50), a leading magnate such as Lord Cromwell at Wingfield Manor (1440s), and the King at Hampton Court Palace (1532–5).

THIRTEENTH-CENTURY DEVELOPMENTS

By the opening of the thirteenth century a lordly residence included a dominating hall, a chamber for privacy, a chapel for worship and the associated kitchen and services within a walled or fenced enclosure, sometimes protected by a moat. The ancillary domestic units of stables, bakery, laundry and workshops would be irregularly grouped within or without the gated enclosure but, as these structures were less well-built and frequently timber-framed, they have rarely survived.

Initially, the position of the entry into the hall varied between the gable-end

Donington le Heath Manor, Leicestershire. The upper chamber block of a moated manor house of c.1280 with its first-floor doorway from the lost hall. The house was much altered and extended in the early seventeenth century.

Clarendon Palace, Wiltshire. The foundations of the outer walls, the bases of the aisle columns, raised dais, and gabled end wall of the late twelfth-century hall, built by Henry II. The foundations of the royal apartments, services and kitchen have also been excavated and left exposed.

(Westminster, Caen) and a side wall (Richmond, Oakham). By the start of the thirteenth century the doorway was regularly positioned in the side wall at the low end of the hall, enabling a formal progression to be made towards the upper or high end where the owner and his family sat, be he king, lord, or small landowner. But owners found that traversing the length of the hall after a meal to reach their personal rooms over the services was inconvenient, and so the two functions of the chamber block were separated. The family rooms were built next to the upper end of the hall while the services continued to be relegated to the lower end. During the thirteenth century, therefore, there were several planning developments, reflected in many of the hundred or so houses that have survived:

– the practice was adopted of two opposing entrances at the low end of the hall, together with the creation of the cross-passage between them, screened from the hall to give it some privacy from the multifarious activity it engendered;

– the position of the service rooms for the provision of food was consolidated with a high-quality chamber above, though the kitchen continued to be a stand-alone building, as a precaution against fire;

– the location of the owner's private chambers to the rear of the high table provided more effectively controlled access, while the already noted extension at Merton Hall points to the growth of the family unit with one or two wings to enhance its facilities and comfort.

Already the words 'low' and 'high' are replete with symbolic and hierarchical meaning and this aspect will be developed much further during the later Middle Ages.

The most complete thirteenth-century aisled halls stand within Bishop Auckland Palace (County Durham) and Winchester Castle, though now lacking any associated chamber blocks. Both retain their tall aisled columns and arcaded arches but with remodelled gabled windows and replacement roofs. That in County Durham possibly dates from the early thirteenth century rather than the more usually ascribed later twelfth century and is still in use, though as the bishop's chapel since the 1660s. The Winchester hall, begun for Henry III in 1222 and completed in 1235 at a cost of over £500, makes decorative use of Purbeck marble for the slender columns which divide the hall into five bays. There are two small service doorways at the lower end and an elaborate one at the opposite end leading to the (destroyed) royal apartments. This hall has survived as a result of its use as a courtroom from the thirteenth century to the late twentieth.

As the hall was the focal point for all meals, the erection of buildings for their provision was a natural corollary of hall development. In larger households the services were usually divided into two, a room for storing ale and wine (the buttery, derived from the Anglo-French *butt*, a large wine cask) and one for storing bread and other dry goods (the pantry, from the Anglo-French *panis*, bread). These formed the basis of a household's diet and were originally held in one or more detached units. Once these functions were brought under the hall roof, a two-storeyed unit was a natural corollary as it enabled a residential chamber to take the additional upper space over the two service rooms. However, the kitchen continued to be detached to avoid the danger of fire spreading to other parts of the house. The low end of the hall was therefore usually marked by three doorways, often grouped together, serving the buttery

Bishop Auckland Palace, County Durham. The Bishop of Durham's magnificent early thirteenth-century hall was converted into a chapel in 1666, when the roof was raised with its line of high windows.

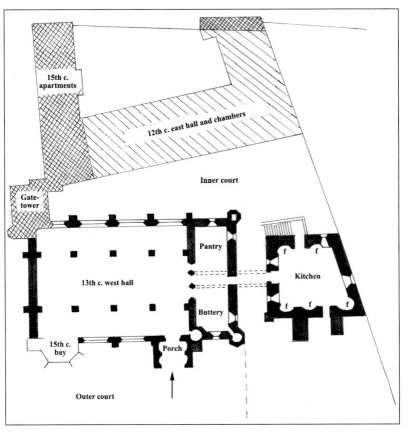

Lincoln: Bishop's Palace. Ground plan of west hall, services (with great chamber over), and kitchen.

and pantry respectively, with the central entry opening into a passage leading to the detached kitchen. A fourth doorway and stair close to the hall entry would access the residential chamber above the services. The use of this apartment was neither fixed nor regular – it could be allocated to guests, the parents or eldest son of the owner, the steward or a senior household official.

Though badly mauled, the ruined great or west hall of the Bishop's Palace at Lincoln is an early example of this service area development (*c.*1190–1210). The three associated doorways are well preserved in the lower end wall of the aisled hall, with a newel stair by the entry porch accessing the state chamber above the services (converted into a chapel in 1886 when the doorways below were blocked). The central passageway led to the massive stone-built kitchen with its five fireplaces – indicative of the munificence of this episcopal household. The ruins of Warnford Manor (*c.*1220) in Hampshire is another early example of the hall and end unit plan, as is the very grand example of *c.*1280 by Bishop Burnell, Edward I's chancellor, at his palace at Wells.

Lincoln: Bishop's Palace. The richly decorated doorways to the buttery, pantry and central kitchen passage. They were blocked in 1886.

Lincoln: Bishop's Palace. The entry porch added to the Bishop's hall shortly after its completion. The rich mouldings and inclusion of black Purbeck marble columns made a statement of the Bishop's wealth and status.

Lincoln: Bishop's Palace. Because of falling ground, the detached kitchen was necessarily built over a vault to bring it up to the same level as the hall. The tiled back of one of the fireplaces is exposed.

The halls at Oakham Castle, Clarendon Palace, and the Bishop's Palace, Lincoln, all have a single entry, but two opposing entries became far more convenient and standard practice from the mid thirteenth century onwards. They can be seen in the halls at Winchester and the contemporary manor house at Ashby de la Zouch, Leicestershire (it only became a castle two centuries later), and subsequently at Nassington Prebendal Manor House (*c*.1280–90) in Northamptonshire and the bishop's hall at Wells, similar in plan and scale to the earlier royal hall at Winchester. Continuous movement and domestic activity at this nub of a house meant that the cross-passage was usually screened from the hall, but, because it was of wood, few early examples have survived. Enough fourteenth-century examples exist to suggest that the practice had developed earlier, concurrent with the cross-passage form.

Wells, Somerset: Bishop's Palace. Bishop Burnell's development of c.1290 was on the grandest scale. Only the outer wall of the hall survives with its line of magnificent windows, but the still-used chapel at the high end of the hall is virtually a glass box.

Martock, Somerset: Treasurer's House. The much smaller hall of the mid fourteenth century abuts the lower end of the mid-thirteenth-century cross-wing. Because the house has been continuously inhabited, the primary early features are limited to a gable-end window with painted glass, surrounded by contemporary wall-paintings of a Crucifixion scene of c.1260. The gable-end hall window shows that the family continued to occupy the lower end of this house throughout the Middle Ages.

Plaxtol, Kent: Old Soar. The aisled timber-framed hall (site to left) has been destroyed, leaving the central chamber block flanked by the lower roofed wings of the chapel (with end window), and the garderobe block.

Hall and services under a common roof led to a vast roofed area, as at Lincoln Palace and Nurstead Court (Kent, *c.*1314). It was not a major step to create a more flexible solution in large-scale buildings by roofing the services unit at right angles to the hall instead of in line with it. The benefit of extending the services beyond the line of the hall to create larger rooms at ground level as well as at the upper level was quickly appreciated. The cross-wing plan became increasingly common from the mid to late thirteenth century, as at the Treasurer's House, Martock (Somerset, *c.*1250–70). The benefit of this development at the lower end of the hall was equally applied from the mid thirteenth century onwards to the upper end, where the two-storeyed cross-wing was swiftly adopted to create the increasingly common H-shaped plan exemplified at Charney Bassett Manor House (Oxfordshire, *c.*1280). The manor house at Ashby de la Zouch is an example of where the upper cross-wing was added during the early fourteenth century to an existing hall and low end unit to enhance the privacy of the Zouche family.

Whereas Ashby is ruined but retains its hall and family unit, two splendid thirteenth-century chamber blocks stand roofed and floored but without their associated halls. Old Soar, Plaxtol (Kent), is a fine example of an upper chamber block of *c.*1280–90 with its south-west face carrying a decorated corbel that formally supported the arcade of the destroyed hall. The ground floor and upper floor of the block are similar in plan – a central vaulted room with two diagonal projections, which served on the upper floor as a bedchamber with garderobe and chapel respectively. It is likely that the chapel

Little Wenham Hall, Suffolk. Developed between 1265 and 1280, when the manor was held by Sir John Vallibus, this chamber block was built of flint and local seashore stone as well as brick, with dressed stone for the windows and doorways. Note the generous first-floor windows compared with the narrow loops of the two vaulted ground-floor rooms.

projection is a slightly later addition to the withdrawing chamber, while the presence of several arrow loops shows that security-needs cannot be totally discounted even as late as Edward I's reign.

Even more impressive is the slightly earlier Little Wenham Hall (Suffolk), of *c.*1265–80. Like Boothby Pagnell, this chamber block stands in the grounds of a nineteenth-century house. This well-designed L-shaped building is not only a rare example of brick construction dating well before its common use in the fifteenth century, but it displays the highest architectural standards. The first-floor chapel is a jewel, with its vaulted ceiling, striking window-flanked entry, carved sedilia, piscine, and candle brackets, as well as a generous east window. Again, a security element cannot be discounted when the house was moated, embattled and crowned with a third-storey tower high above the roof line. The absence of a hall and the presence of a large heated first-floor chamber have led past commentators to assume Little Wenham was a prime example of a first-floor hall house. However, the position of four otherwise unexplained doorways at the unbuttressed south-west angle suggest that the (probably) timber-framed hall lay to the south, with two of the doorways opening into an adjacent garderobe projection serving both floors.

The present halls attached to a considerable number of chamber blocks are often later, as in the Essex manor houses at Little Chesterford and Tiptofts

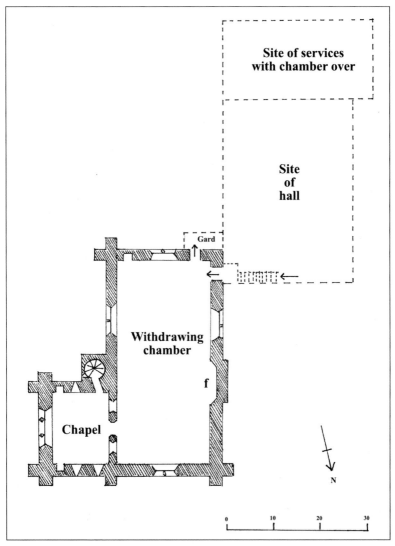

Little Wenham Hall: first-floor plan. (The scale of the hall and services block is based on Tiptofts Manor, near Saffron Walden.)

(probably both late thirteenth century), because the original wooden structures were subsequently replaced in stone or timber when it became necessary to give the house a more up-to-date character. Thus the late twelfth-century chamber block at Irnham Hall (Lincolnshire) is attached to a mid-fourteenth-century stone hall, though the latter includes the ghost of its predecessor. At Temple Manor, Strood (Kent), the documentary evidence of 1308 referring to the hall, *camera*, and chapel was confirmed when excavation revealed evidence of an early fourteenth-century timber hall built against the north wall of the standing

Acton Burnell, Shropshire. Whereas part of Bishop Burnell's hall survives at Wells, his hall at Acton Burnell does not, leaving only this imposing chamber block of the 1280s. It was on the grandest scale, as befitted Edward I's chancellor and his wealth from eighty-two acquired manors. His standing and friendship with Edward I enabled him to entertain the king and his retinue when parliament was held here in 1283.

Acton Burnell. The ground floor of this chamber complex was divided into two large and two subsidiary chambers for staff, with the Bishop's apartments on the upper floor. They consisted of a well-lit private hall, centrally arcaded, with three linked rooms, including a substantial one at attic level. Though close to the Welsh border at a time when the king was subduing central and north Wales, Burnell's personal accommodation was non-defensive and markedly comfortable.

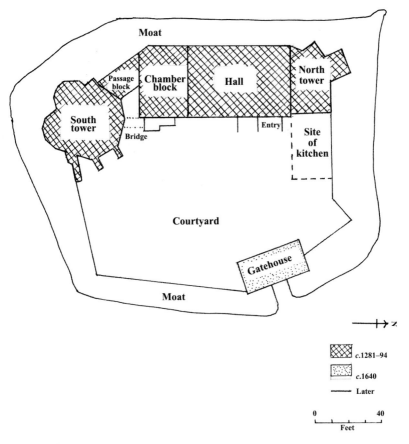

Stokesay Castle, Shropshire: ground plan.

stone chamber block of 1225–50 (the *camera*). It was surmised by the excavator that the original twelfth-century hall was also a timber one. The stair approach to the family apartments was also extensively rebuilt. These family rooms were initially newel-approached, as in the Lincoln and Plaxtol examples, but a straight flight of stairs gave a more grand and formal approach. These were initially external but an enclosed stair rising from the high table of the hall was soon preferred.

The defendable house at Stokesay (Shropshire) stands as a summation of house development during the closing years of the thirteenth century. Built between 1284 and 1296 by a leading wool merchant based in Shrewsbury, the central hall with its gabled windows is flanked by the two-storeyed offices to the right (plus the lost kitchen against its blank wall) and the external-stair approached solar block. The whole range stands in line with the end units in cross-wings to the hall, evidence of tiled floors, painted wall decoration, fireplaces with hoods, and an original internal stair of the 1280s to the north

43

Stokesay Castle, Shropshire. This fortified house of a Shropshire wool merchant has hardly been altered since the late thirteenth century. This view from the north shows the projecting timber-framed upper floor contemporary with the remainder of the house and which provided generous domestic accommodation. The ornate timber-framed gatehouse in the background was built well over three centuries later. The moat was initially water-filled.

Stokesay Castle. Built of local stone, the three-windowed hall is flanked by the upper and lower chamber blocks in a classic layout. Traces of lime render suggest that the whole structure may have been whitewashed originally. Note that the solar window was stepped to avoid the lost roof above the stair to the private apartments. This house should be compared with the contemporary residence similarly built not far from the restless Welsh border at Acton Burnell (page 42).

Stokesay Castle. The hall was always the principal room of a medieval house but this one at Stokesay also retains evidence of its wall plaster, whitewash and painted decoration. The upper half of the windows was glazed but shuttered below. The roof is an early example of a cruck structure developed at a time when the elimination of intrusive aisle posts to clear the floor space left only vestigial evidence in the end walls.

tower. The family accommodation was lavishly extended shortly after completion by the addition of the multi-windowed south tower. The whole was wall-enclosed and moated, with the gatehouse replaced in 1640 by the present highly decorative timber-framed entrance. This courtyard house impresses with the generosity of its accommodation within a comparatively small area, the wide span of a hall without aisles, and the comfort demanded by the owner.

4. Architectural developments: 1300–1500

During the fourteenth century the number of significant houses held by the leaders of society gradually declined. Edward I inherited twenty houses from his father and although this number rose to twenty-five early in Edward III's reign, it had fallen to seventeen by the close of the century, to twelve under Henry VI and to ten with the advent of Henry VII. The same downward trend applied to the episcopacy and aristocracy. The Bishop of Hereford held at least thirteen houses at the opening of the fourteenth century, but the decision was made in 1356 to limit the number to seven. During the same period Aymer de Valence, Earl of Pembroke, had castles at Haverfordwest (Pembrokeshire), Pembroke, Goodrich (Herefordshire) and Sutton Valence (Kent), residences at Moreton Valence (Gloucestershire), Newton Valence (Hampshire), Inkberrow (Worcestershire) and Hertingfordbury (Hertfordshire), and he built a new house at Bampton in Oxfordshire. Yet we have records of him visiting Bampton only twice, in 1307 and 1312, and virtually nothing to indicate that he travelled to Pembroke or Haverfordwest. The restriction of long periods of occupation to two or three houses is one of the key changes in residential development during the fourteenth century. It arose, in part, because peripatetic travelling to use up the crops and resources of an estate was no longer efficient or necessary, and also from the realisation that all those resources needed to be husbanded so that they could be lavished on a handful of properties to achieve the necessary scale

Ludlow Castle, Shropshire. A classic example of hall and cross-wing development. The first-floor hall and lower cross-wing, both above low undercrofts, were erected by the Lacy family between 1283 and 1292. Shortly afterwards, the cross-wing was heightened to provide superior accommodation. Between 1309 and 1328 the luxurious double chamber block was added at the upper end of the hall (right) by Roger Mortimer, Earl of March, paramour of Edward II's queen.

of magnificence. In addition, higher living standards made it financially prohibitive to bring houses of earlier generations up to date. And in the particular circumstances of the crown, this reduction in the number of residences was also a consequence of the centralisation of government at Westminster in the mid fourteenth century. During the later Middle Ages, therefore, not only was the peripatetic lifestyle practised during the twelfth and thirteenth centuries replaced by an essentially static one, but households became larger and privacy became more important. The architectural consequence was that houses became more complex.

HALL MODIFICATIONS

The hall with its high roof continued to be the centre of domestic life but its form was modified and its function changed during the later Middle Ages. Probably the most important structural development was the elimination of aisles to create an uninterrupted open area, but other changes enhanced the apartment's comfort and style through the introduction of bay windows, wall fireplaces and elaborate screens.

Nearly two hundred aisled halls with timber or stone columns have been identified from visible evidence, excavation and documentary research. They extend from royal and episcopal palaces to relatively modest dwellings but were essentially limited to lowland England and more particularly to the most populous parts of the country – the sweep of south-east England from Suffolk to Hampshire (though a late and anomalous group has been identified in central Yorkshire from the fifteenth and sixteenth centuries). Aisle posts or columns cluttered the internal space, made more obvious by the growth in household size. And while the aisle bays had often served as sleeping accommodation, the development of staff lodging ranges during the fourteenth century hastened

Penshurst Place. Sir John Pulteney's entry porch makes a fine preface to his hall of 1338–49, compared with that planned but not built at Ludlow Castle. Note the boldly decorated hall windows descending almost to the ground with relieving arches above that help to carry the thrust of the hall roof (see page 80).

47

Penshurst Place. The north porch was intended to impress a visitor with its tierceron vaulting, quatrefoil-decorated entry arch, original oak door and wicket door for daily use. The side benches have been inserted later, for they make it difficult to reach the door to the upper chamber stair (right).

their elimination. The aesthetic and practical benefits of their much desired removal occurred relatively swiftly during the first half of the century. The Bishop of London's conservative hall at Nurstead Court (*c*.1314) was one of the last major aisled halls in England, while the 35 feet (10.7 metres) wide structure of 1325–35 built for the Archbishop of Canterbury at Charing Palace (Kent), only 25 miles away is an early example of the fully cleared hall. Space clearance was greatly facilitated by contemporary experiments and improvements in roof construction carried out by a number of master carpenters in different parts of the country. This movement was initiated by raising the roof on massive tie beams, cambered to give them greater strength and capacity to transmit the roof weight on to the walls, although this was merely one of several methods used to clear the hall floor with the consequent heightening of the side walls. This complex subject is further discussed below but it enabled fourteenth-century élite halls

Penshurst Place. The hall of c.1340 has been little altered. The screen incorporates medieval elements but is essentially late sixteenth-century and later. The floor tiles and central hearth are at least sixteenth-century and may be even earlier.

Gainsborough Old Hall, Lincolnshire. The hall louvre allowed the smoke to escape from the central hearth. The best-preserved example in England, it was taken down in 1950 for reasons of safety and is now kept within the building.

such as those at Mayfield (Sussex) and Penshurst Place to be at least 39 feet (11.9 metres) wide and that at Kenilworth Castle over 45 feet (13.7 metres) wide.

The central hearth had been a constituent element of halls at all social levels since earliest times, frequently positioned nearer the high table than the lower end. Though the heat would have been most welcome, the smoke could have been equally distressing, making it virtually essential for halls to continue to be open to the roof. In larger houses, the smoke from hall and kitchen escaped through a lantern or louvre on the apex of the roof, but gaps at eaves level are not unknown. Timber-framed louvres survive from the hall at Gainsborough Old Hall (Lincolnshire), and above the kitchen at Stanton Harcourt (Oxfordshire). Considering that wall fireplaces occur in Anglo-Norman houses, the continuing practice of central hearths, as at Penshurst Place (1341–9) and Padley Hall (Derbyshire, *c.*1425), is surprising, though smoke-covered timbers are often the only indication of a former central hearth today. Yet they continued in the largest halls such as Wingfield Manor (1443), Eltham Palace, London (1475–80), and Hampton Court (*c.*1532), long after wall fireplaces had become common, suggesting a symbolic significance. For wall or mural fireplaces had developed during the fourteenth century, usually in a side wall of the hall as at Brinsop Court (Herefordshire, *c.*1340), but occasionally heating the dais

Howden Manor, Yorkshire. This country residence of the Bishop of Durham on the road to London was built by Bishop Skirlaw in about 1390. Only the hall and entry porch survive. The hall was tall and well-windowed like that at Penshurst but it was radically altered in the eighteenth century when it was converted into a two-storeyed house.

against the upper end wall (Dartington Hall, Wressle Castle, both of c.1390). Initially fireplaces were hooded to help control the smoke (Aydon Hall, Northumberland; Meare Manor Farm, Somerset) but low-arched or square-

headed fireplaces were usual by the mid fourteenth century. They were surmounted by lintels of increasingly decorative character towards the close of our period (Tattershall tower-house; Muchelney abbot's house, Somerset). By this time side wall fireplaces with external projecting stacks were a standard updating to replace the central hearth of earlier halls, as at Haddon Hall and Ightham Mote.

From the thirteenth century the body of the hall had been dignified by the regular placing of windows in nearly

Howden Manor. This chaste Yorkshire porch is a contrast with the southern richness of that at Penshurst Place. It is broader but similarly vaulted and with a well-moulded entry doorway. The side benches are original.

Kenilworth Castle, Warwickshire. The first-floor hall of 1372–80 built by John of Gaunt, Duke of Lancaster, above a vaulted undercroft has deep floor-to-roof windows, opposing wall fireplaces and a broad entry arch leading to the Duke's private apartments.

every bay, as at Stokesay Castle and Northborough Manor (Cambridgeshire). Usually the windows were shuttered and lacked glass except in the decorative traceried head, but glass became more common in high-status houses during the fifteenth century, often enhanced with painted arms and heraldic devices (Ockwells Manor; Lyddington Palace, Rutland). The practice also arose during the fifteenth century of positioning the windows in the upper register of the wall to allow for the solid walling below to be filled with expensive tapestries, or painted cloths for those unable to afford the highly prized Flemish hangings. The weaving of tapestries had developed during the last quarter of the previous century and they had quickly become a highly valued status symbol. Tapestries were probably hung below the hall windows at Wingfield Manor and Eltham Palace (now with a modern replacement hanging), while Tickenham Court (Somerset, *c*.1470) is a more modest example where the windows of the earlier hall were modified to keep up with the latest developments.

Lighting the upper end of the hall with projecting or bay windows became popular during the fifteenth century. They occur, as might be expected, in those vanguard buildings John of Gaunt's Hall at Kenilworth (*c*.1372) and that built by Edward IV at Eltham Palace, but also in medium-sized houses such as Elsing Hall (Norfolk) and Athelhampton Hall. Opposing bays opening from broad moulded arches were particularly popular in the Somerset/Wiltshire area, as at South Wraxall Manor, Great Chalfield Manor and Hazelbury Manor, all adopting the practice of one of the bays opening on to the stair to the family apartments. Bays were also added to earlier halls to improve the dais lighting (Tickenham Court) or to provide a more imposing stair accessing the private apartments (Penshurst Place, Haddon Hall).

A further practice for dignifying the position occupied by the lord and his family at the upper end of the hall was to erect a canopy over the dais. This

Great Chalfield Manor, Wiltshire. Built between 1478 and 1485, this watercolour of the hall interior by J. C. Buckler in 1823 shows the high-set windows, wall fireplace, stone side benches and the screen shielding the cross-passage and open door to the parlour.

could be of fine fabric but has rarely left any trace of its existence so that we have to rely on manuscript evidence for its presence or the rare survival of hooks (Wingfield Manor) or pegs (Tattershall tower-house). But wooden or plaster canopies have sometimes survived post-medieval floor insertions and other changes, particularly in the north of England. Those at Rufford Old Hall (Lancashire, c.1500) and Adlington Hall (Cheshire, c.1505) are highly elaborate. Those to the east of the Pennines in Yorkshire are less so, as at Horbury Hall (1470s), Shibden Hall (late fifteenth century), and Thornhill Lees Hall (early sixteenth century). Fewer have survived in the south but can be identified at Framsden Hall (Suffolk, later fifteenth century), and in several smaller timber houses in the south-east.

Wooden screens at the lower end of the hall are more frequent, though equally vulnerable to removal and decay. Fragments remain of that in Eltham Palace hall, sufficient for a full reconstruction to be made in 1933, and the same occurred at Great Chalfield Manor, though the surmounting 'musicians' galleries' in both examples are an anachronistic Tudor feature. Some of the earliest screens are in the north and west, where the narrow cross-passage at the lower end of an aisled hall is marked by a roof truss with the aisle width plaster-filled to form a solid screen or 'spere' – hence the term 'spere truss'. Fourteenth-century examples survive in the north-west at Smithills Hall, Bolton, and Baguley Hall near Wythenshawe, in the Welsh borderland at Amberley Court in Herefordshire, in the west Midlands at West Bromwich Manor House (Staffordshire) and Little Malvern Court (Worcestershire). The open central area would be filled with a massive screen, as in the relatively

52

plain mid-fifteenth-century survival at Chetham's, Manchester (now secured to the ground), though the movable examples at Samlesbury Hall (Lancashire, 1532, but now broken up), and the slightly earlier one at Rufford Old Hall are riotously carved. The more usual type of screen was that fixed to the side walls, with either a single central entrance or two openings, usually in line with the service doorways. Such screens, heavily restored, can be seen at Ockwells Manor and Cothay Manor (Somerset), totally restored at Haddon Hall, brought from elsewhere at Berkeley Castle (Gloucestershire), or remade at Dartington Hall. Screens were more likely to be elaborated on the hall side than towards the cross-passage to emphasise the importance and dignity of the dais end.

During the late fourteenth and fifteenth centuries the hall became the apartment for receiving guests formally and with ceremony before proceeding to the private apartments. It was still used for feasts, banquets and entertainment but far less for daily dining, so that its pivotal role started to diminish towards the close of our period. Not all medium-sized houses wished to have such a large formal apartment so that halls began to be restricted in scale at the expense of the cross-wing, and more particularly of the family private rooms. The date for this change has not yet been fully explored but evidence for it can be identified in Somerset during the mid fifteenth century. At Wells Palace, Bishop Beckington built a house for himself separate from the formal episcopal apartments of his predecessors, with the hall no longer open to the roof but low-ceiled and surmounted by his withdrawing chamber. Near-contemporary examples in the region occur at Gurney Manor and Gothelney

Manchester: Chetham's. The fifteenth-century hall of this college of priests is one of the best-preserved in northern England. It retains its original 7 feet (2.1 metres) high oak screen of three equal sections with two broad openings (curtained).

Wells, Somerset: Bishop's Palace. One of the most memorable medieval residences in England, with its four-phase development immediately spelt out. The central residential block was built during the early thirteenth century (nineteenth-century dormer windows), with the chapel and ruined hall added in the late thirteenth century. The precinct was enclosed with an embattled gatehouse (see page 162) and towered walls (behind the camera) in the mid fourteenth century, while the more domestic-looking house on the left was added in the mid fifteenth century.

Hall, together with Ashbury Manor in Oxfordshire, built in *c.*1480 by the monks of the abbey at Glastonbury, 6 miles from Wells. The movement can also be identified in East Anglia by the last quarter of the fifteenth century, though this reduction in hall size did not spread to Kent until the first decade of the sixteenth century. The few large halls that continued to be built open to the roof during Henry VIII's reign were those of the crown (Hampton Court Palace) or by members of the court (Cowdray in Sussex, Cotehele in Cornwall) for reasons of status.

ROOF STRUCTURES

As in churches, two of the most decorative features in a medieval house are the differing forms of window tracery and roof construction. Both help us to date a building as their form changed over the years, but window size and tracery variation did not affect house development to the same extent as roof techniques.

Considerable energy has been devoted since the 1950s to the analysis and categorising of roof structures, with the minutiae of minor examples and technical variations threatening to overwhelm subject clarity. This section is therefore limited to the two fundamental roof types from about 1100 to 1500, with the earlier possibly reflecting influence from northern France.

Common rafter roofs were spanned by a line of identical or common rafters, secured at the base into a wall plate (the horizontal beam forming the head of the wall). Although there might be a tie or cross beam spanning the side walls, there was no ridge member and these roofs lacked longitudinal stiffening. As a consequence, racking occurred, that is the distortion and movement caused by the lack of sufficient strengthening to resist high winds and gales. To help overcome this, many early roofs have a plethora of bracing. Domestic examples before 1250 are very few, because of destruction or replacement, so that the majority of common rafter roofs today are ecclesiastical – cathedrals, churches or barns.

The problem of racking was resolved during the mid thirteenth century when rigidity was introduced through longitudinal timbers called purlins which gave support to the common rafters. Further stability was provided by pairs of much larger or 'principal' rafters, which demarcated the covered space into bays. At the same time, 'wind' braces spanning each bay were secured to the back of the rafters. This second key type, the *principal rafter roof*, was particularly favoured in western and northern England.

Not surprisingly in a country of considerable regional variation and with master carpenters known for their structural ingenuity, there are several sub-sections of both forms, named after their most distinctive structural member. In a brief account such as this, only one variation of each form can be described, but they can often be seen in high-status houses. Crown-post roofs were a development of common rafter roofs, while hammer-beam roofs were essentially a development of principal rafter roofs.

Crown-post roofs were initially found in south-east England with the common rafter structure strengthened by a tie beam supporting a central vertical post, or crown post, to a higher collar trapping a longitudinal timber known as the collar purlin. This gave the roof much greater stability than before. There are several variations following the development of such roofs, with early examples visible in the refectory of Bushmead Priory (Bedfordshire, *c.*1250), the hall of the Old Deanery, Salisbury (*c.*1260), and the solars at Charney Bassett Manor House (*c.*1280), and Old Soar, Plaxtol (*c.*1290). Crown-post roofs became characteristic of lowland England and, as these examples illustrate, they were not limited to halls but were favoured for all important rooms in a house.

Plaxtol, Kent: Old Soar. The solar is an elegant and lofty room with window seats, pegs for shutters, and part of the original stone floor next to this window. The brick floor covering the remainder of the room is probably sixteenth-century. The roof is of crown-post collar-purlin design.

Lytes Cary, Somerset. This mid-fifteenth-century hall has high arch-braced collars springing from angel corbels holding shields with the Lyle family arms. It is given distinction by the highly decorated wall plates immediately above the windows of pierced quatrefoils linked by undercut tracery, and three tiers of wind braces.

As tie beams can rarely span a width greater than 32 to 35 feet (9.8 to 10.7 metres), the solution to roofing larger halls without aisle posts was resolved by a development of the later thirteenth century. The *hammer-beam roof* not only enabled much wider roof spans to be created, but it facilitated a highly decorative covering to the most important apartment in a house. Visually rising in stages, the tie beam is replaced at that level by a short beam (the hammer beam) projecting from each side wall, supported by a curved brace. From the end of the beam, a post (the hammer post) rose to the braced collar at the higher level. Whereas a tie beam holds the side walls together from the outward stress of the roof weight, a hammer-beam structure works on the cantilever principal. The earliest known roof of this form is that spanning the Pilgrims' Hall in the cathedral close at Winchester (*c.*1290) but it occurs in a domestic context shortly afterwards at Tiptofts near Wimbush and at Upton Court, Slough (both *c.*1330). The most famous hammer-beam roof is that built in combination with massive arch braces at Westminster Hall, London, by Hugh Herland between 1394 and 1399. The form had already become popular in high-status buildings, probably at Kenilworth Castle and certainly at Dartington Hall, and during the fifteenth century at Crosby Place, London (1466), and Eltham Palace hall (1480). Hammer-beam roofs continued to be used for high-status buildings throughout the sixteenth century, sometimes in double hammer-beam form, as at Giffords Hall (Suffolk).

HOUSE EXPANSION

During the first half of the fourteenth century the fully developed H plan – a central hall with family and service cross-wings – became widespread across the Midlands (Haddon Hall, Ludlow Castle) and southern England (Stonor Park, Oxfordshire, and Penshurst Place), followed by the north-west later in the century (Beetham Hall, Preston Patrick Hall, both in Cumbria). The plan was favoured because of its flexibility at a time when more accommodation was being sought to

Ightham Mote, Kent. The moat, entry arch (originally drawbridge-protected) and the ground floor of the range to its right are work of the 1330s. The gatehouse was raised in c.1480 at the same time that the upper part of the linking ranges was timber-framed. They were re-faced in stone and re-windowed in the early seventeenth century. The bridge is of late date.

meet the need for family privacy and household expansion. The development of Ightham Mote near Sevenoaks illustrates the thrust of this development.

This moated house was probably built by a member of the Inge family during the 1330s using stone (hall and chapel) and timber framing (two solars) in a

Ightham Mote. The principal court of c.1331–45 with stone hall (right), two timber-framed solars (centre), and framed guest lodging of c.1480 above a formerly open loggia (left).

combination that was repeated throughout the property's extended development. Dendrochronology has shown that building was not initiated with the hall but with the two blocks of family apartments (1330 and 1331) and the entry gateway (1332), followed by the hall (1337) and chapel block (1342). Though the hall was conventionally heated by a central hearth, the two contemporary blocks of family apartments were an unusually generous initial provision. Ightham Mote also reflects a stage in the formalisation of a house's layout – a more regular ordering of the subsidiary buildings within the perimeter enclosure. Though further ranges were added round the courtyard in the 1470s, there was a staff range outside the drawbridge-protected entry from the house's inception.

The extensive increase in cross-wings roofed at right angles to the hall is particularly evident during the later fourteenth and fifteenth centuries, especially in the development of the upper cross-wing beyond the hall dais. The ground-floor chamber was used for various purposes (storage for clothes, luxury goods, or for lesser family accommodation) but above was the great or

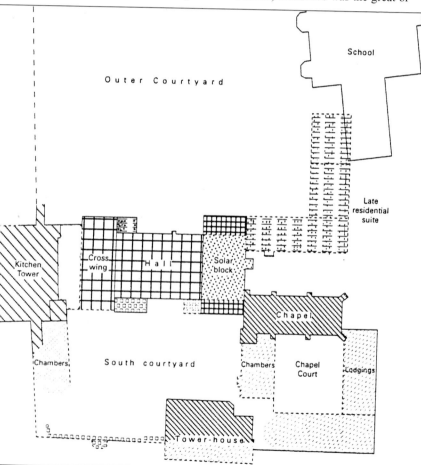

withdrawing chamber, where the family spent much of their personal time. This was a multi-purpose apartment serving as bedroom, retiring room, family and privy chamber until these functions were separated into a suite or group of rooms. This seems to have been the case with the two solars at Ightham Mote. At Ashby de la Zouch the early fourteenth-century chamber block was extended at both ends a hundred years later when the two ground-floor rooms were given independent entrances from the outer and inner courtyards respectively, while a new stair led to the magnificent 68 feet (20.7 metres) long withdrawing chamber, with its enriched fireplace and lofty end windows. Henry V's brother John, Duke of Bedford, added a linked building in *c.*1430 to the mid-fourteenth-century great chamber at Penshurst Place. With the new work showing evidence of French influence, the principal floor consisted of a suite made up of a lobby, an outer and inner chamber, and a closet, in a sequence of increasing privacy. At Haddon Hall, the mid-fourteenth-century chamber block was enhanced at both levels in *c.*1490 when the ground-floor room was upgraded as a 'parlour' with a new end window and painted ceiling of chequer

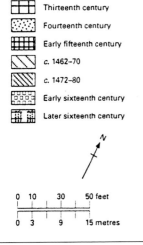

Thirteenth century

Fourteenth century

Early fifteenth century

c. 1462–70

c. 1472–80

Early sixteenth century

Later sixteenth century

N

0 10   30   50 feet

0   3   9   15 metres

Ashby de la Zouch Castle: site plan.

Ashby de la Zouch Castle, Leicestershire. The fourteenth-century withdrawing chamber, above two low ground-floor rooms, was extended at both ends in the early fifteenth century. The fine chimneypiece with its enriched lintel was added at that time but the enormous end window is a Tudor enlargement of the earlier one.

and diaper pattern with heraldic emblems, while the family chamber above was given a new roof and timber-framed extension of private rooms (page 88).

The fifteenth century was the period when the word *parlour* came into fashion. It applied to a superior ground-floor room, usually at the upper end of the hall, as at Haddon Hall, where it could be used privately or for dining by the family. It was one of the developments that reduced the significance of the hall. But at Great Chalfield (1478–85) the low-end services were also replaced by a formal room, its high status emphasised by a wall-painting of a corpulent man

Penshurst Place. This mansion was sold to John, Duke of Bedford, Henry V's brother, in 1428. He added the impressive range in extension of that built by Sir John Pulteney seventy years earlier (right). It was essentially a private first-floor suite above low ground-floor rooms, with staff attic rooms above (mid-Victorian dormer windows).

Great Chalfield Manor. The late fifteenth-century manor house built by a lawyer, Thomas Tropnell, is fronted by the moat of the previous dwelling. The plan of the house is simple but the balanced composition is one of receding planes from the bold cross-wings to the central hall. The wings are emphasised by the first floor oriels; they are not identical.

wearing an ermine-trimmed gown, a crown or beaver hat, and carrying what looks like a large money bag. It may be a portrait of the builder, Thomas Tropnell. The chamber above had also become an important one, enhanced by an oriel comparable to that lighting the formal withdrawing chamber beyond the upper end of the hall. Visitors can appreciate the attractiveness of such chambers here and at Cothay (1485), still in use, though furnished in keeping with present-day rather than medieval comfort.

Both these houses illustrate the later development of the *lower cross-wing*. Though the room above the services had continued to serve a useful but secondary purpose for guests, the in-laws or household officials, the pressure for converting it to prime accommodation became overwhelming if that at the upper end of the hall was already fully developed through site restrictions. This can be seen at Ightham Mote, where a new kitchen was built during the 1470s at the south-east corner of the house, next to the fourteenth-century one, so that a new high-status chamber could be added over the original kitchen. The practice was repeated on a more impressive scale at Ashby de la Zouch (c.1462–70) and slightly later above the services at Cotehele. The lower end of the hall was no longer seen as an inferior area of the house. Detailed regional work suggests that cross-wing enhancement during the later Middle Ages extended across the country – from Cumbria and the West Riding of Yorkshire, through the south Midlands and the Vale of White Horse to the Kentish Weald. It is a striking testimony to the coherence and unity of the gentry class in England, while the frequently repeated assumption that the north trailed behind central and southern England architecturally is not borne out by such evidence.

Any household of standing possessed a *chapel* or oratory and usually a chaplain. Their existence is one of the primary elements distinguishing a superior house from that of modest social status. Bishops' registers are full of requests from the more affluent for a licence for mass to be celebrated in their house, particularly those some distance from a church. They are a valuable resource for dating existing structures or identifying those in lost houses. Chapels varied from the imposing examples at Little Wenham and Broughton 'Castle' (Oxfordshire, *c*.1310), to the tiny fifteenth-century oratory at Gurney Manor, which could hold only the priest and three participants. A number of little-touched examples survive in south-west England, in Somerset at Clevedon Court (*c*.1320) and Blackmoor Manor (late fifteenth century), in Devon at Bradley Manor (1425) and one of superior quality at Compton Castle (*c*.1450), and in Cornwall at Cotehele (late fifteenth century), which retains its original altar cloth. Where no structural evidence of a chapel survives in large-scale mansions such as Dartington Hall and Wingfield Manor, then one can be postulated in areas now demolished, particularly if there is documentary evidence for its existence, as there is at Dartington in February 1400.

Chapels grew in scale commensurate with the growth in households. That at Old Soar, Plaxtol, is modest. The one at Woodlands Manor (Wiltshire, *c*.1330) is more elaborate, with the evidence of an external stair (in addition to internal family access) for staff or neighbours. In these and most other examples the chapel was usually sited next to the family apartments. Those at Ightham Mote and Cotehele had a shuttered window to allow the family to partake in services without entering the chapel. From the late fourteenth century chapels might have a balcony for family use, with staff in the body of the room, as in the Yorkshire examples at Bolton Castle (*c*.1380–90) and Calverley Hall (*c*.1485–95), and The Vyne near Basingstoke in Hampshire (1518–28). Such chapels were usually positioned at ground level but in modest houses they

Bradley Manor, Devon. This early fifteenth-century house is low-built, with the projecting chapel on the right added in 1427. The house was re-fronted in the late fifteenth century.

Ashby de la Zouch Castle. The kitchen is a detached structure of 1462–70. The uppermost rooms above the work area were well-windowed, with seats, fireplaces and lavatories, indicating that they were apartments of substance.

Right: *Ashby de la Zouch Castle. The kitchen filled two-thirds of the tower's full height. The vaulted work area includes a well, a double fireplace, a single fireplace, hatches and the remains of a serving table and wall cupboard. The destroyed east wall included a further major fireplace.*

might be above the porch, as at Cothay Manor (c.1485) and Ashbury Manor (c.1488), where the chapel retains its wooden screen separating it from the withdrawing chamber. Detached chapels within the courtyard offering a facility to local parishioners are not infrequent, as at Hall Farm, Bentworth (Hampshire, c.1340), and West Bromwich Manor House (late fifteenth century), for chapels can be among the least touched domestic rooms to survive, as at Horne's Place (Kent, two-storeyed, c.1360), Rycote (Oxfordshire, 1442), and Hendred House, East Hendred (Oxfordshire), which has been in unbroken use since the mid thirteenth century.

Kitchens were frequently detached structures to protect against fire and to cope with the staff numbers and activity involved. Nearly all those that survive

Gainsborough Old Hall. The kitchen, brick-built in 1462–70, was initially separated from the body of the hall by a small open court. It was filled to create a servery in c.1480.

are square and stone-built, though it is surprising how many records refer to timber-framed structures, as at Stokesay Castle. The thirteenth-century example at Weoley fortified house south of Birmingham was a rectangular building, 41½ feet by 22½ feet (12.6 by 6.9 metres), with a central hearth and weatherboarded walls. Two late medieval examples were originally timber-framed but subsequently either stone-cased (at Martholme in Lancashire, possibly sixteenth century) or brick-cased (at Wonston Old House in Hampshire, possibly fifteenth century). Otherwise there are at least fifty survivals, with striking examples still in comparable use at Dartington Hall and Stanton Harcourt (both late fourteenth century), complete at Haddon Hall (mid fourteenth century and initially independent), as well as at Gainsborough Old Hall (1462–70) and (though ruined) at Ashby de la Zouch and Wingfield Manor. Many of those still serving meals in collegiate foundations such as Eton College, and New College, Oxford, retain considerable evidence of their early form and facilities, as do those in some of the grandest mansions, such as Durham Castle, with its hearths and serving hatches, or Windsor Castle, where the remodelled roof structure of 1362–3 looks down on the highly modern facilities used for state banquets.

COURTYARD HOUSES

The prevalence of the H plan for superior house planning extended from magnate residences (the castles at Ludlow and Bamburgh, Northumberland) to gentry and some merchant-financier town houses (Crosby Place, London) as it percolated lower down the social scale. However, those of the highest status needed more facilities than this form offered to accommodate all the members of the household. The reasons for this will be discussed in chapter 9 but the consequence was the expansion of the cross-wings to form the quadrangular or courtyard plan.

It is highly arguable whether the domestic courtyard developed from the castle bailey or the monastic cloister. It is likely that they both contributed to a basic characteristic of military, ecclesiastical and residential design, with the fortified house serving as a bridge between the fortress and the domestic house. By the beginning of the fourteenth century the courtyard was the primary shape for most high-status houses, such as Penhallam Manor in Cornwall, where the excavated sequence of rooms was built round the perimeter of an earlier moated ringwork, terminating in a gatehouse and drawbridge of *c*.1300.

The earliest domestic entrances were more like *gateways* with a room over, rather than a gatehouse, which suggests a more military structure. This was the form at Northborough Manor (*c*.1335), Steeton Hall (Yorkshire, *c*.1360) and Baddesley Clinton (Warwickshire, *c*.1526–9), where the entry gave privacy, status and possibly protection from marauders and threatening neighbours. *The Paston Letters* show why some East Anglian gateways were embattled and provided with a portcullis or gun-loop during the fifteenth century, as at Oxburgh Hall (*c*.1482) and the contemporary Elton Hall (Cambridgeshire). But at the same time late medieval gateways gave a more imposing and dignified entry to a house, as in the low-standing examples at Tretower Court (Powys) and West Bower Manor (Somerset), or the taller examples at Hadleigh Deanery (Suffolk), Layer Marney Towers (Essex), and the contemporary colleges at Oxford and Cambridge.

Baddesley Clinton, Warwickshire. A moated house of multi-period construction. The rear has evidence of a mid-fifteenth-century residential block but the gateway and front ranges are a rebuilding of the late 1520s.

At first, the ranges round a *quadrangular courtyard* were built against its outer walls, providing a line of lower (ground-floor) and higher (first-floor) status accommodation, as at Maxstoke Castle (Warwickshire, 1342–6), and the reconstruction of the upper ward of Windsor Castle by Edward III. Here the extensive royal accommodation was developed round three small courts to fill one side of the ward (1357–63), with the household ranged round two further sides (1364–77) against the earlier towered walls of the ward, with the fourth side closed by the remodelled keep (1353–7) on its earlier motte (illustrated on page 108).

By the second half of the fourteenth century, unencumbered sites enabled the ranges to be integrated with the walls to create a more regular form of enclosing ranges round a central court, as at Dartington Hall, built between 1388 and 1400 by Richard II's half-brother, John Holand, Earl of Huntingdon. Opposite the entrance block stands the great hall, flanked by three-storeyed cross-wings and a detached kitchen. The two extended sides of the court are filled with lodging ranges (illustrated on page 129) to create a regular and imposing quadrangle like that of contemporary collegiate foundations such as Winchester College and New College, Oxford, to which the concept is not unrelated. The same development can be seen in the north of England. The Neville family, for instance, rebuilt their castles at Brancepeth (*c.*1360–80) and Raby (*c.*1367–90), both in County Durham, on the plan of towers and apartments irregularly grouped

Southwell Palace, Nottinghamshire. The state chamber is a fifteenth-century rebuilding of the more modest upper chamber of this episcopal residence. In the distance is the east gable-end of the contemporary chapel, part of the palace extension round an inner court.

Haddon Hall, Derbyshire. The fourteenth-century hall and chamber block were developed and extended throughout much of the fifteenth century, when the whole house was turned round. What was the rear court became the entry court, as shown here, when the porch and fireplace stack were added to the earlier hall.

round courtyards. Within a few years, the family had adopted a more formal quadrangular plan with integrated ranges at Sheriff Hutton in Yorkshire (1382–1402), as the Percy family did at Wressle Castle (1390–1403), not far away.

Whereas a single courtyard was adequate for most households, *two courtyards* became desirable in the larger residences. Some fortresses had always had an outer and inner courtyard for defensive reasons and to provide lines of protection, but the form did not develop in residential architecture until at least the late thirteenth century, when it was an element of the two largest episcopal palaces in London, Lambeth Palace and Winchester House. One of the earliest country houses to adopt the double-courtyard plan was Dartington Hall, shortly after 1388, where there is standing and excavated evidence of a small, irregularly planned second court. The standing evidence is a gallery of *c.*1475-83 but the paucity of the family accommodation without the second court (particularly the absence of the documented chapel of 1400), its irregularity and some early excavated pottery suggest that the origin of this second court lay in the closing years of Richard II's reign, although the execution of John Holand in 1400 probably precluded development completion. Contemporary examples of double-courtyard planning include the Bishop of Chichester's manor house at Amberley (Sussex, 1377–83), Scotney Castle (Kent, *c.*1378–80), and Farleigh Hungerford Castle (Somerset, *c.*1370–83), while the form had become the norm for high-status houses by the second quarter of the fifteenth century, as at Southwell Palace (Nottinghamshire,

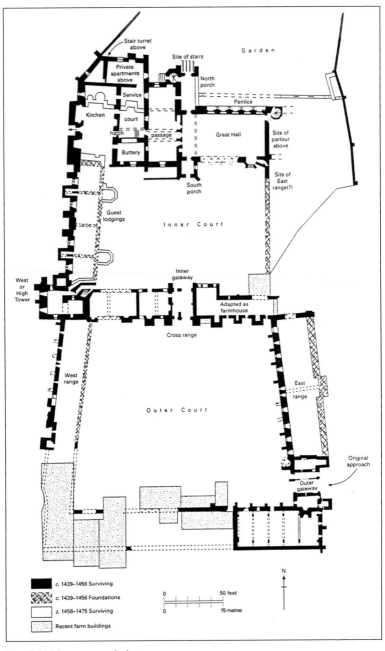

Wingfield Manor: ground plan.

Wingfield Manor, Derbyshire. The ruined hall retains most of its walls, porch and bay window but has lost the three-storey complex of private rooms beyond its upper end (right). However, it retains a second suite of private apartments tiered above the services, including the richly windowed audience chamber (left).

c.1430–50), Wingfield Manor (1439–56) and Haddon Hall (mid fifteenth century). The two courtyards were nearly always separated by the hall, facilitating the distinction of an outer court for services and an inner court for the private apartments of the householder. The outer court was more open to the world and had greater public access. The inner court encouraged privacy, the development of secondary or inner chambers and even suites, and gave greater control over access. Triple courtyards occasionally occur during the fifteenth century (Sheen Palace, Sudeley Castle, Hampton Court near Leominster), as did multiple courtyards. Externally, Herstmonceux Castle (Sussex, c.1438–49), looks complete but its four-courtyard interior was regrettably swept away in 1771 and can be recovered only from plans made shortly before its destruction. The same applies to Eltham Palace, stripped of its multiple courtyards to leave only Edward IV's hall (1478–83) as evidence of its continual royal favour throughout the later Middle Ages.

Single-courtyard planning filtered down the social scale, primarily applying to defendable residences in the north, such as Ford Castle under Sir William Heron (1338), Chillingham Castle under Sir Thomas Heton (1344), and Workington Hall under Gilbert Culwen (1380–1400). Courtyard houses were less defensive in the Midlands, as at Cheyney Longville (Shropshire, c.1395) by Sir Hugh Cheyne, Treago Castle (Herefordshire, c.1470) by Sir Richard Mynors, and Baddesley Clinton (mid fifteenth century) by John Brome. Those

Haddon Hall. The fourteenth-century hall retains its original windows and service doorways but the screen is a mid-fifteenth-century replacement.

in East Anglia and the south were entirely residential, such as Oxburgh Hall (1482) by Sir Edmund Bedingfield, South Wraxall Manor (Wiltshire, late fifteenth century) by Henry Long, and the development of the Deanery at Wells under John Gunthorpe (1472–98).

This and the previous chapter have shown that the thread of hall, a family room, kitchen and offices stretches unbroken from at least the eleventh century to the still recognisable form of entry hall, living room and kitchen of suburban houses today. Though these units were initially detached, their conjoining in a single structure is the first critical phase in the architectural development of houses in England and Wales. The years close to 1300 initiated the second stage in the story of domestic architecture with the expansion of this all-important core and the addition of further discrete units reflecting the increasing wealth and developing hierarchy of late medieval society. Some of these developments were structural while others were cultural, particularly the desire for privacy, or political (see later). These chapters close at the point when the third critical phase of house development was fostered under the Tudors and Stuarts – the reversal from inward-looking to outward-facing structures which no longer reflected internal functions. During the sixteenth and early seventeenth centuries windows were punched in hitherto unbroken external walls and regularised, courtyards were opened up, and balanced façades became standard, surmounted by 'swagger' chimneys. As form took precedence over function, multi-windowed houses gave no indication of the internal layout while passages and corridors, staff stairs and smaller rooms improved circulation and privacy. But that story is for another author.

5. Building materials

It is clear to anyone who travels round England and Wales that there is an extremely close relationship between the geology of the country and the materials used to create the rich cornucopia of medieval buildings that we enjoy. These materials extend from the famous stone quarries of the limestone belt and the oak woods of Kent and Sussex to the flint outcrops and thatching reeds of East Anglia. These are lovingly described in *The Pattern of English Building* (1987) by Alec Clifton-Taylor, whose knowledge, scope and enthusiasm have not yet been superseded.

After the Conquest, cathedrals, churches and monasteries were built of stone, castles made use of timber as well as stone, while houses spanned the broadest range of building materials, which included bricks from about 1400 onwards. It is this variety of materials that gives so much pleasure when visiting the houses of any period, whether in the countryside or in a town.

STONE

Timber was far more plentiful than stone in Anglo-Saxon England, though the survival of stone churches at the expense of timber buildings has distorted the picture. Even so, the legacy of stone building under the Anglo-Saxons was improved by their discovery of lime mortar to bond the courses together. Mortar mixers were discovered close to the stone-built royal palace excavated at Northampton (early ninth century), though there is otherwise little evidence of extensive secular masonry building before the Norman Conquest.

Such activity vastly developed in the century or so following the Conquest, hastening the expansion of a substantial pool of craftsmen as well as one of unskilled labour. Furthermore, the extent and quality of the work involved in some of the largest projects – royal works, leading monasteries and private fortresses – meant that there was now a capable resource for building stone houses.

This movement of master masons and an effective labour force to serve the many substantial projects helped to disseminate building skills across the country, culminating in the massive castle-building operations of Edward I in north Wales, where the manpower resources of up to five thousand (quarrymen, diggers, scaffolders, carpenters, masons, smiths and tilers) conscripted between 1277 and 1283 were drawn from almost every county in England. As work continued for the next fifty years, this influx of novel methods and resources had a dramatic influence on local building practices. Such projects, albeit on a more modest scale, by others over generations in different parts of England and south Wales helped to develop regional skills and local styles. Building work was seasonal, usually extending from March until November, though the records for Kirby Muxloe (1480–4) show that adverse weather conditions could shorten this.

Though the Normans initially imported stone from the area near Caen in Normandy for some of their most important buildings (the Tower of London; Battle Abbey, Sussex), they rapidly appreciated that England was rich in high-quality building stone. In particular, there is a wide range of colour, textures and weathering properties in the deposits quarried from the great Jurassic limestone belt that extends from Lincolnshire and Northamptonshire to Gloucestershire and south Dorset. The stone houses that were built from the mid twelfth century onwards are found as much in towns (Lincoln and Southampton) as in the countryside (Boothby Pagnell, Burton Agnes).

As the demand for masonry building accelerated and continued unabated throughout the later Middle Ages, there was a substantial increase in more local stone quarrying. It was prompted as much by stone's stability and permanence compared to timber as by the development of a professional labour force and emulation of the more wealthy properties. Using such quarries cut down transport costs and made it possible to extend a building in the same texture and material as before. It is often difficult to locate these quarries today as they have usually been exhausted and either backfilled or left as overgrown dumps, but local quarries provided the majority of building material, at Markenfield Hall, Yorkshire (limestone), Cotehele, Cornwall (granite) and Thornage Hall, Norfolk (flint). Ashlar (dressed stone) was usually used for quoins (corner stones), chimneypieces and window and doorway dressings to give greater style and detailing to a building (Lyddington Palace), even if it meant bringing that particular material some distance. The decoration of the hall of the Bishop's Palace at Lincoln was enhanced by the importation of Purbeck marble from south Dorset, while the dark, bluish limestone quarried on the south Devon estate at Dartington to build the hall there was offset with cream-coloured ashlar for windows and doorways brought from Beer in east Devon. Beer stone was also used in the construction of Richard II's apartments at Portchester Castle though the majority of stone in this royal development was brought from quarries in the Isle of Wight. Changes in architectural detailing including mouldings, reliefs and sculptured shaping as detailed in Margaret Wood's *The*

Markenfield Hall, Yorkshire. An extremely well-preserved moated house near Ripon expanded from a more modest dwelling by John Markenfield, a self-made man and Edward II's chancellor from 1310 to 1312. This view shows the buttressed first-floor hall above an earlier undercroft, with fine windows separated by the chimney stack. The end lavatory projection served the private apartments. The house was a grander version of the slightly earlier Aydon Castle.

Cotehele, Cornwall. The use of local stone over several centuries has made it difficult to determine the several building phases of this romantically situated house overlooking the river Tamar. Built between 1470 and 1520, this range exhibits two types of material. Sir Richard Edgcumbe (died 1489) used a rough brown and grey slatestone with ashlar dressings for his early residential range, while Sir Piers Edgcumbe (died 1539) changed the approach by inserting a three-storeyed entry tower using cut granite blocks.

Cotehele. The hall court retains the original entry to the house (left) and chapel east window, tightly abutting the end of the family range (centre) and hall (right). The entry range and chapel are earlier than the hall and apartments, which were rebuilt by Sir Piers Edgcumbe in about 1520 with distinctive window and door heads.

Lyddington Palace, Rutland. This much altered residential range of one of the Bishop of Lincoln's country residences is built of dark honey-coloured ironstone rubble with limestone dressings and Collyweston slates. It is essentially a late fifteenth-century remodelling of an earlier structure with fine first-floor apartments above relatively low staff rooms.

Dartington Hall, Devon. This imposing late fourteenth-century kitchen, built of local stone and originally free-standing, was a roofless ruin until restored in 1937. It retains two massive hearths in adjoining walls, tall windows and a doorway to the lost second court (foreground area).

English Medieval House (1965) can be far better appreciated in stone than in timber or brick.

TIMBER

The paucity of workable stone in certain areas of England and Wales made the use of timber essential. However, since the mid twentieth century the study of timber-framed buildings has extended beyond typological and regional variations to the abstruseness of joint techniques and the minutiae of differing roof structures. Unfortunately, technology and detailing have sometimes become an intellectual end in themselves rather than an illumination of the broader framework.

The early development of timber framing in Britain is still subject to considerable discussion but a major change seems to have occurred by the beginning of the thirteenth century when the earlier practice of earthfast posts, i.e. the positioning of timbers directly upon or into the ground, was replaced for all major buildings by the introduction of the sill beam. This was the horizontal timber lying on or surmounting the low perimeter wall of the building, and into which the timber posts were mortised. The introduction of the sill beam was crucial for the development of timber framing, for the superstructure became dependent on close-fitting joints for its stability. Earthfast posts would rot and were unable to support heavy roof structures unaided. Stone (and later brick) footings supporting the sill beam not only gave much greater life expectancy to the structure but their combination with squared timbers and jointing techniques brought strength and rigidity. The development of joint techniques to withstand intense stresses and support complex structures has a literature of its own, but one crucial factor was the introduction of the pegged mortise and tenon joint. This is found in very few buildings before the close of the twelfth century, but it is almost ubiquitous by the close of the thirteenth century. Even so, only a small number of thirteenth- and fourteenth-century timber-framed houses have survived compared with those from between the later fifteenth and eighteenth centuries. It should be borne in mind that this was not necessarily because there were so few of them. The decimation of the population as a consequence of the plague during the mid and later fourteenth century brought violent upheavals and depopulation throughout the country, leading to the abandonment of many houses. Timber structures were more susceptible to decay than stone and often left no more than a moated site as evidence of a formerly thriving household.

Oak was used for nearly all structural members of a medieval house. Ash and elm were occasionally used for low-status buildings from the sixteenth century onwards, though Yelford Manor (Oxfordshire)

Baguley Hall, Manchester. One of the earliest timber-framed houses in north-west England. The framing was raised on low sandstone walls and characterised by massive horizontal and upright timbers. The three service doorways (two blocked) dominate the lowest plane, with a line of trefoil and quatrefoil cusped braces above. The spere truss separating the hall from the cross-passage lacks the central free-standing screen that survives at Chetham's, Manchester (see page 53).

Little Moreton Hall, Cheshire. This is one of the few timber-framed houses in north-west England that has been subject to detailed analysis. The hall (centre) and upper cross-wing (left) were erected by Sir Richard Moreton between 1440 and 1450. The more patterned lower cross-wing (right) was the work of his son. Both wings were elaborated in about 1559. Painting the timbers with black pitch or paint to create a magpie effect was unknown before the late eighteenth century.

of 1499–1500 was built of elm from the nearby woods. But timber framing in England and Wales developed along two different paths. The introduction of the continuous sill led to the development of box framing. However, the Midlands and Welsh borderland also developed the entirely different system of cruck framing, though there was much overlapping between the two types, as well as a range of structural developments over an extended period of time.

One of the major advantages of *box framing* was that it could be prefabricated on the ground, usually near the construction site, with the timbers cut and numbered to ensure correct assembly. This practice enabled more complex and efficient joints to be developed than was possible when the structure had been fully assembled. When the outer frame had been erected on the sill, then internal cross-frames could be introduced to divide the building laterally into bays. The floor frames were inserted and the roof added to complete the structure. It is the joints that give the structure the rigidity necessary to withstand the forces that might distort it – the loads it has to support (extending from people to stored goods and heavy roof tiles) and the wind forces that might rack it. The complex roof structures that are among the greatest pleasures of a timber-framed building were often purposed to meet these structural problems rather than for aesthetic reasons. Box framing was particularly popular in eastern England south of the Humber, southern England and the Welsh borderland.

The second fundamental form of house carpentry was *cruck framing*. Two pairs of timbers, usually curving inwards, are positioned to meet at the apex of the roof so that a line of them gives the fundamental strength to support the added outer walls and the weight of the roof. The latter is carried to the ground by the crucks, not by the outer walls, which are for weatherproofing, practical and aesthetic purposes only. All cruck trusses support a ridgepiece and are usually stabilised and locked together by a collar. The form seems to have originated in the west Midlands and spread towards the Welsh border and central Wales, northwards to Cumbria and north Yorkshire, and towards south-west England. It also extended eastwards until it met the alternative structural form of box framing with posts and tie beams. But cruck frames and box frames are not mutually exclusive. They can be found not only within the same region (e.g. north and central Wales, the Vale of White Horse) but also in the same village (e.g. Harwell, Oxfordshire). Cruck houses have been dendro-dated from the mid thirteenth century, with an acceleration during the later fourteenth and fifteenth centuries until the sixteenth century, when the form was on the wane. Though some cruck buildings are of relatively high status and well carpentered (the hall at Stokesay Castle), it was not a form adopted by those of the highest rank.

BRICK

In contrast to stone and timber, brick is a man-made material. Roman bricks were often a ready source for reusing in early churches, but freshly made bricks were used in early medieval Suffolk and Essex, a region of particularly poor building materials. Brick initially tended to be limited to coursing or vaulting in conjunction with other materials, as at Coggeshall Abbey (*c*.1225), but Little Wenham Hall (*c*.1280) is an outstanding example of its employment on a substantial scale.

Brick making and brick building on a large scale were developed at the close

of the thirteenth century, centred on Hull. Brick was used to construct Holy Trinity Church (*c*.1315–70) and the town walls at Hull (1321–1400), the magnificent gatehouse at Thornton Abbey in Lincolnshire (*c*.1382) and the striking tower-house at Tattershall in the same county (*c*.1440), four architectural highlights of the region. The bricks at

Tattershall Castle, Lincolnshire. Lord Cromwell's tower-house of the mid 1440s is one of the most striking secular achievements of late medieval England. Standing in almost complete condition, the brickwork is offset by the stone dressings, particularly on this show west front. The plan is common throughout of one great chamber on each floor with vaulted closets in the three angle turrets and the stair in the fourth.

Faulkbourne Hall, Essex. A spectacular brick-built house, mainly attributable to Sir Thomas Montgomery in 1462–75. His range of private apartments terminates in a regnal tower of contrasting shape and scale. The quality of the brickwork is outstanding in a residence that eschews contrasting stonework. It includes plain and multi-moulded brickwork and a distinctive corbelled and embattled parapet unifying a building that was originally larger.

Tattershall were made at Edlington Moor, 9 miles away, though bricks were more usually made in kilns as close to the building site as possible.

A much higher standard of workmanship had been achieved by the second quarter of the fifteenth century, not only in making bricks of more consistent shape and colour but through developing a far greater range of decorative detailing. Although nothing survives of its use for Henry V's palace at Sheen, the high standard attained by 1443 can be seen in the gatehouse at Rye House, where the diaper patterning, corbel tables and friezes necessitated over fifty different types of moulded brick. By then, brick was becoming a fashionable material, chosen by Sir Roger Fiennes for his moated palace-mansion at Herstmonceux, followed immediately afterwards by Henry VI for Eton College. Where the crown led the baronage and gentry quickly followed, as at Faulkbourne Hall (in two phases between c.1430 and 1470), Farnham Castle gatehouse (1470–5), Buckden Palace tower-house (1472–80), Gainsborough

Buckden Palace, Cambridgeshire. A country house of the Bishops of Lincoln, remodelled in brick by Bishop Rotherham (1472–80) and his successor, Bishop Russell. The former began the tower-house (right), which was completed by the latter, who erected the moat-protected gatehouse to the inner court. Their work gave a defensive air to buildings that were entirely domestic in character and purpose.

Gainsborough Old Hall, Lincolnshire. The approach to this house illustrates the use of timber and brick in a high-status residence, with the family range (right) and central hall of 1462–70 and the lodging range (left) of 1479–85. However, the earlier work was initially entirely of timber-frame construction, the present ground-floor brickwork being post-medieval and Victorian replacement.

Old Hall (*c*.1478–85), and Kirby Muxloe Castle (1481–4). Such activity culminated in its preference by the first two Tudor monarchs for their palaces at Richmond, Greenwich and Hampton Court.

Throughout this period patrons of the new material were limited to the crown, magnates, leading ecclesiastics and court officials. Even so, brick structures were essentially confined to eastern England, and more particularly to the region east of a line extending southwards from the Humber estuary through the mid Thames valley to the Sussex coast, with a single outlier at Repton in Derbyshire (*c*.1440). Foreign craftsmen, particularly Flemings, are recorded in

Gainsborough Old Hall. The north side of this mansion reveals the stone bay window inserted in the earlier framed hall in about 1580 (using earlier materials) and the residential brick tower fashionably added by Sir Thomas Burgh to his earlier house in 1479–85. The tower rooms were for Burgh's personal use.

building documents from the early fifteenth century onwards (e.g. Stonor Park, 1416–17) but the extent to which they influenced or dominated brick making in England is still under discussion. There is a marked contrast between the highly decorative 'foreign' features and detailing used in the tower-house at Faulkbourne Hall and the much plainer English character of Herstmonceux Castle. Flemish brickmakers were employed at Farnham and Kirby Muxloe castles, but this influence seems to have tailed off after *c*.1485. By the early sixteenth century there was a large body of English brickmakers in southern and eastern England, many of them employed in the ever increasing portfolio of royal works.

OTHER MATERIALS

The further range of building materials is extensive. Slate was indigenous to Cumbria, south-west England and much of Wales and was particularly useful for roofs, while far more houses were covered with thatch or shingles than have survived today. The Purbeck Hills of south Dorset provided the marble that was so highly prized for embellishment between the late twelfth and fourteenth centuries (Winchester Castle hall), though Frosterley marble was used in north-east England (Bishop Auckland Palace hall). Plaster was not limited to covering internal walls but was sometimes used to cover external stonework (Giffords Hall gatehouse, *c*.1500). Even such a humble material as cob has been found at Bowhill, a wealthy merchant's country house of *c*.1500 outside Exeter. But it

Penshurst Place, Kent. This and the next roof are a study in contrasts, separated by two centuries. That of the hall at Penshurst of c.1340 spans an apartment of considerable width (39 feet; 11.9 metres). To achieve this, the full-size figures (formerly standing on corbels) supported massive trusses (arch-braced collar beams), from which the central crown post rose to the roof ridge. Both end gables carried high windows that helped to illuminate the roof.

Cotehele. The hall of c.1520 was only 22 feet (6.7 metres) wide but the apartment was given majestic scale by its height and the decorative moulding of the arch-braced trusses, with their feet curving down the wall, and the four lines of intersecting wind braces. Note the contrast between the deliberate darkening of these timbers and the untouched character of those at Penshurst Place.

is the combination of local materials that provide some of the happiest visual ensembles. Patterned brick or colour-washed plaster infilled the framing of timber houses, while the junction of stone and timber at Ightham Mote has already been noted. It also occurred at Stokesay Castle, Wingfield Manor, and later at Chorley Hall (Cheshire), but Giffords Hall combines timber framing and plasterwork with both flint and brick in one of the most harmonious houses to have survived from late medieval England.

Most building industries were closely localised to their source of raw materials but even they could be subject to fashion and status. Sophisticated carpentry was initially demonstrated in several early medieval aisled halls, but as stone became more fashionable for the aristocracy from the twelfth century onwards, so did its cost. Transporting Taynton stone from near Burford in Oxfordshire sixty miles to Windsor added considerably to Edward III's expenditure on the castle. The cost of carrying the golden iron-tinted stone from Ham beyond south Somerset was warranted because it contrasted so well with more prosaic local materials. It was a similar contrast that had previously made Purbeck marble so fashionable and expensive. Locally made brick became prized only from the early fifteenth century as a consequence of higher standards of consistent shape and colour and innovative decorative qualities. Royal patronage by Henry V at Sheen Palace (1414–22) and by Henry VI and his queen during the 1440s at Eton College and Queens' College, Cambridge, fostered its wider appreciation and aristocratic popularity.

81

6. Contents and furnishings

The majority of medieval houses in England and Wales are still in private hands, with their interiors essentially reflecting present-day living standards. Carpets, curtains, sofas and electric lights hardly convey a realistic image of a medieval interior. Even where apartments have long been abandoned but retain their roofs, as at Bolton Castle or West Bromwich Manor, floors have been replaced, walls stripped of plaster, and reset glass inserted in the windows. One or two museums and publicly owned properties have sought to reinstate a medieval character through their furnishings. Leeds Castle (Kent) has recreated two early fifteenth-century royal rooms, a great chamber and a bathing room, while the hall and kitchen at Gainsborough Old Hall have been furnished in a manner appropriate to a late fifteenth-century knight's household. Medieval secular interiors have to be drawn primarily from documentary and literary sources, manuscript illustrations, and panel paintings, but these can be supplemented by a number of isolated fittings and furnishings that have survived centuries of use.

Gainsborough Old Hall, Lincolnshire. This fine hall was the centre of Sir Thomas Burgh's house of the 1460s. The hall timbers have been dendro-dated to c.1465 but the stone bay window (left) was an addition of about fifteen years later, remade in Elizabeth I's reign. The hall has been laid out with the lord's chair and table on the dais, with a display of plate nearby, and tables lining the body of the hall, which is embellished with banners and wall-hangings, and was heated from a central hearth.

Wealthy people today are reluctant to display their wealth overtly – it is considered vulgar. Medieval people had no such qualms, any more than the Victorians did. There were no moral, social or political reservations or inverted snobbery about spending money lavishly and openly. The money bags of the Treasurer of England displayed so conspicuously at Wingfield Manor, and the apartments at Tattershall Castle, built by Ralph, Lord Cromwell, who held that post from 1433 to 1443, deliberately drew attention to the source of his wealth. The more public rooms in a house would be decorated with wall-paintings of a didactic nature, such as battle scenes and the representation of heroes, or subsequently by tapestries or wall-hangings. The more private rooms were furnished to impress honoured guests with armorial tapestries, personal emblems or choice *objets d'art*. Owners might or might not be able to read the books they purchased, but they could admire their content and show off the quality of their illuminations.

What we most lack today in looking at medieval houses is colour. A close examination of some cathedrals and churches shows that the loss of polychrome decoration since the Reformation is fundamental to our judgement about their exteriors and interiors. The same is true of England's houses. We lack the banners and hangings that fluttered outside, the rich cloths and textiles that covered the furniture, the tiles and painted glass, the chapel contents, and the personal items that gave rooms richness and individuality. Wooden roofs and corbels would be brightly painted while attendants would be wearing embroidered livery. The visual was a vital component of medieval life which is frequently overlooked through concentrating on architectural form.

FITTINGS AND DECORATION

External display was a prelude to internal richness. It frequently took an heraldic or armorial form, ranging from the Percy lion facing the road to

Raglan Castle, Monmouthshire. Part of the well-windowed frontage of the apartments built by Sir William Herbert in c.1460–5, decorated with shields bearing the badges of himself and his wife.

Steeton Hall, Yorkshire. The embattled parapet on all four sides of this gatehouse of c.1360 is supported on a corbel table with a fine display of contemporary heraldry. It includes the arms of the owner, William Reygate, Archbishop Thoresby and several local families.

Scotland on the tower-house façade at Warkworth Castle to the arms of the builder's family at Raglan Castle (Monmouthshire) and Nevill Holt. There is far more figure sculpture in castles and houses of northern England than in the Midlands or south, extending from the arms of the owner and his family at Harewood (Yorkshire) and Sizergh (Cumbria) to displays that included the crown and the arms of prestigious neighbours at Bothal (Northumberland) and Cawood (Yorkshire). Those at Hylton and Lumley in County Durham are particularly spectacular (both late fourteenth-century), reminding visitors where power resided when some northern families were more important regionally than the distant crown. Even the corbel table of the gatehouse at Steeton Hall (Yorkshire, c.1360) is a visual statement of position and influence, more apparent when it was painted or gilded. Other external decoration included elaborate mouldings and window tracery, figurative gargoyles and gable-surmounted beasts (Great Chalfield Manor), ball-flower friezes below the hall eaves (Northborough Manor) and pinnacles supporting armorial weather vanes (Athelhampton Hall).

Internal display often encompassed the mouldings and decoration of doorways, windows and fireplaces, with their richness indicating the importance of the room. Roofs, in particular, were embellished with mouldings

and shaped members to give stature to an apartment. As the most important family rooms were usually at first- or upper-floor level and therefore open to the roof structure, its elaboration and decoration was often purposed to impress.

Most medieval *ironwork* is found in churches and cathedrals, extending from decorative strapwork on doors and chests to grilles and clocks. Secular hinges tended to be utilitarian, as is the ironwork on doors, though the scrollwork decorating the entry door to Merton College hall, Oxford, is a rare late thirteenth-century survival. Otherwise, ironwork is limited to an occasional knocker or ventilation plate in a services door (Dartington Hall) and the chapel clock of the 1490s at Cotehele.

The windows in the most important domestic rooms – the hall and withdrawing chamber – would be glazed, but often only in the upper lights. The

Lyddington Palace, Rutland. The fourteenth-century audience chamber of the Bishop of Lincoln was remodelled in the late fifteenth century, when it was re-windowed and inset with painted glass. Although the chamber had originally been open to the roof, the beam and panel ceiling was inserted at the same time to enable an attic floor to be created above. The ceiling was embellished with a delicate cornice of tracery fans and a vine-trail frieze below.

lower ones would be barred with iron and shuttered for ventilation. With few exceptions, only the chapel windows would be fully glazed. *Glass* was translucent rather than transparent, white rather than clear, with domestic stained glass limited to royal residences before its use in leading houses during the fifteenth century. Heraldic glass was usual, with figured glass limited to the chapel (e.g. Hampton Court near Leominster). We have very little early domestic glass but the material from that period usually combines armorial designs with badges and mottoes, as at Ockwells Manor (1450s), highlighting family and neighbouring connections. This similarly occurs at Athelhampton Hall and Lyddington Palace (*c.*1500). Norbury Hall (Derbyshire) retains several roundels illustrating the labours of the months (1480) while the contemporary hall bay window at the Commandery, Worcester, is filled with animals, birds and plants. For those who could not afford glass, thin sheets of horn were used as window panes until the sixteenth century.

Early *floors* were either beaten earth or chalk, as in the hall of the Old Deanery, Salisbury, or covered with a fine spread of mortar. Flagged floors were laid where there was a local supply of suitable material, as in many Cotswold houses, though hand-made tiles for flooring were common from the early thirteenth century onwards. The simplest tiles were plain, but heraldic designs predominated in a domestic environment, with some of the earliest on display in the ruins of the first refectory of Cleeve Abbey (1271–2). As was the case with externally carved arms and those in stained glass, the tiles at this and other properties served as a further reminder of the link between the owner and his patrons and leading families. The oldest secular tiled floor discovered so far is at Clifton House, King's Lynn (*c.*1325), while slightly later examples in their original position survive in the muniment rooms at Winchester College and New College, Oxford. One of the most complete floors was removed from the house of the Bristol merchant William Canynges (*c.*1470) in 1913 and is now in the British Museum, while the tiles from the Duke of Buckingham's palace-fortress at Thornbury (Gloucestershire, *c.*1510–21) are among the most elaborate heraldic displays to survive from the later Middle Ages.

Wainscot or *wood panelling* took over from wall-hangings as a feature of important apartments at the close of our period but little enough remains. Wainscot was used as early as the thirteenth century in royal palaces such as Clarendon and Woodstock (both destroyed) but among the earliest survivals is the later fifteenth-century flushed panelling in the Courtenay Chamber at Maidstone Palace. Within fifty years, fine-quality linenfold panelling was installed at Thame Park (Oxfordshire), Nether Winchendon House (Buckinghamshire) and The Vyne, near Basingstoke, precursors of a popular Tudor feature.

More secular *wall-paintings* survive than was formerly believed, nor are the recent discoveries necessarily a pale shadow of their former colour and form. Initially, the whitewashed plaster-covered walls of high-quality chambers were enhanced by red lines imitating stonework (Wells Palace) though fourteenth-century scrollwork can be seen in the buttery to the hall of Stokesay Castle. But the paradigm of fourteenth-century wall paintings is those covering the walls of the great chamber at Longthorpe Tower near Peterborough. Attributed to about 1330 in the house of a local gentry family, they depict biblical, didactic and secular subjects in a common context, enriched with inscribed scrolls and Latin

Longthorpe Tower, Cambridgeshire. Early in the fourteenth century a residential tower was added to an earlier hall and chamber block. Shortly afterwards the principal chamber, 16 feet (4.9 metres) square, was decorated with paintings that covered every inch of walling. Dated on stylistic ground to the early 1330s, they are a unique domestic interior of a fourteenth-century family of means and taste.

texts. For the Thorpe family, it must have been like living inside the pages of an illuminated book. Equally richly decorated are a private room and lobby built for Edward III in the Rose Tower of Windsor Castle. Completed in 1366, the walls are decorated with an elaborate repetitive pattern of roses set in flowery borders against a crimson-covered background.

Religious subjects do not necessarily mean ecclesiastical ownership of a property, for part of an Annunciation has been uncovered on the gable-end of the withdrawing chamber at Fiddleford Manor, probably built and decorated by the mid fourteenth century for the Sheriff of Dorset. Similarly, a fifteenth-century Resurrection was painted above the contemporary hall dais of Littlehempston Manor (Devon). The mixture of secular and religious subjects occurs at Cothay Manor (c.1485), where the hall paintings include the hanging and funeral procession of Renard the Fox, while one of the private chambers was decorated with a representation of a local saint. At Belsay Castle the original fourteenth-century scrollwork was overpainted with a second scheme in two tiers during the mid fifteenth century, depicting a naval scene above a line of heraldic shields hung from trees against a floral and wooded background imitating a millefleurs tapestry. As wall-paintings were cheaper and more durable than tapestries, they came to be imitated in houses lower down the social scale, as at Bramhall Hall (Cheshire) and Cullacott near Bodmin. The knights painted between the hall windows at Penshurst Place had given way to a detailed painting of the house's builder at Great Chalfield Manor (c.1480).

Haddon Hall, Derbyshire. The fourteenth-century ground-floor chamber was re-formed as a parlour in c.1490, when the end window and checker-board ceiling were inserted. The panelling and frieze were added fifty-five years later.

But it is the parlour at Haddon Hall that was the harbinger of the future when its beamed ceiling was covered with painted decoration of compartmentalised badges and shields on a chequered ground (*c.*1490) and the room was panelled a few decades later.

FURNISHINGS

During the medieval period, furniture and furnishings had a symbolic as much as a practical significance. Furniture, in particular, spoke of an owner's estate and standing, with items such as a cupboard or a chair as an adjunct of ceremony and the household's social structure. Medieval furniture was rarely elaborate, partly because it was covered with expensive textiles and cushions, but also because it needed to be easily dismountable so that it could be moved from house to house.

Not surprisingly, very little domestic furniture has survived six or more centuries of use and hardship. What has survived tends to be *stone furniture* rather than that of wood. Stone window seats are common, though they would have been softened with cushions and fabrics. Low stone benches occasionally remain, as in the hall of Harewood Castle, but stone tables are extremely rare. Fragments of the thirteenth-century marble table from Westminster Hall are kept in the nearby Jewel Tower, while the window embrasures of the prior's hall and chamber at Wenlock Priory (Shropshire) retain their original fifteenth-century stone tables on moulded pillars. Stone wall cupboards are not uncommon, though nearly always lacking their original door and any internal shelf. Stone washing basins were usually positioned near the entry door, as at Wingfield Manor and Lyddington Palace, with more decorative examples at Battel Hall (Kent) and Dacre Castle (Cumbria). Sideboards were even more elaborate, such as those serving the dais at Harewood Castle or the bishop's

Lincoln: Bishop's Palace. The sideboard at the lower end of the Bishop's audience chamber was part of the room's development by Bishop Alnwick between 1436 and 1449. It included a large bay window (marked out by the gravel), fireplace and lavatory.

audience chamber at Lincoln Palace.

No medieval *wooden cupboards* have survived outside those in ecclesiastical hands (Westminster Abbey, Wells Cathedral), while the most famous medieval *chair* is the royal chair of state of *c.*1300 in Westminster Abbey, used at coronation services. St Mary's Hall, Coventry, preserves a mid-fifteenth-century double chair for seating the mayor and master of St Mary's guild, but the only long bench known to the author is that from Barningham Hall held in the Victoria and Albert Museum. Equally rare is the fixed settle of *c.*1500 next to the fireplace in the abbot's parlour at Muchelney, a richly evocative ensemble under a window with retained fragments of contemporary glass.

The privileged area of the hall would be identified by a

Muchelney Abbey, Somerset. The abbot's first-floor withdrawing chamber of c.1470 was a comfortable room, well-lit and with a sumptuous fireplace, with space for a wall-painting above. The oak settle under the windows is an extremely rare survival of c.1500, offset by modern reproduction furniture.

89

Penshurst Place, Kent. One of the two tables in the great hall attributed to the late fifteenth century.

raised dais supporting an extended table at the upper end, possibly with a canopy over the chairs for the owner and his wife. *Tables* would be plain and usually made of boards laid on trestles to facilitate movability. Two such tables stand in the hall at Penshurst Place, attributed to the late fifteenth century, while the remarkable circular table at Winchester Castle hall has been dendro-dated to the late thirteenth century, with its legs cut off in 1348, when it was hung up on a wall, and overpainted in *c.*1520 for the young Henry VIII.

We have to rely on documentary evidence, manuscript illustrations and paintings for an idea of medieval *beds*, for no examples have survived. The frame would be of the simplest form, but it would be as richly draped as the owner could afford. The hangings and bed cover would be lavish, for beds were an item found in withdrawing chambers as well as bedchambers because they were items of dignity and expense. The richest beds had drawn-up canopies of silk or velvet; one has been fully reconstructed and draped at Leeds Castle.

A display of *plate*, made of silver or gold, was a statement of pride and wealth. No medieval royal plate survives apart from two coronation items held in the Tower of London, for it was frequently pawned and much of it was melted down during the Commonwealth. The finest collections of medieval plate are therefore held in those continuing institutions of the medieval world, the colleges of Oxford and Cambridge. Among the more expensive and elaborate items are those given by Bishop Wykeham and his successors to New College, Oxford, and Winchester College, while All Souls College, Oxford, holds a pair of silver-gilt wine flagons with swan handles of *c.*1420 and a spectacular contemporary salt cellar given by its founder, Archbishop Chichele. Less elaborate items are the Studley silver bowl and cover of *c.*1400, possibly used by a noble child to eat from, and the Lacock cup and cover of *c.*1440, which was probably secular before its appropriation by the Church after the Reformation (both held in the Victoria and Albert Museum).

Sculpture played little part within a house except in the chapel. Roof corbels were rarely a display of craftsmanship for they were usually limited to angels and foliage or left plain for painted coats of arms. The stone screen of c.1370–80 in the upper hall of Raby Castle has been badly damaged but retains evidence of the lions' heads, branches and leaves that formerly decorated it. On the opposite side of the Pennines towards Carlisle, Naworth Castle (Cumbria) held three oak figures of the 1470s representing retainers of the Dacre family – a knight, a squire and a man-at-arms – until their transfer in 1999 to the Victoria and Albert Museum. The same applies to the four 6 feet high standing beasts of c.1520 holding reinstated banners taken from the hall of the same castle, heraldic representations of members of the Dacre family. Smaller and less ornate beasts surmount the hammer-beam roofs in the halls at Weare Giffard and Orleigh Court in north Devon.

The loss of colour in medieval houses is underlined by the total absence of *fabrics and textiles*, the victim of usage, wear and tear, and changes in taste. The only secular survival is an early fourteenth-century remnant carrying the royal arms of England, possibly part of a horse cloth, now in the Musée de Cluny, Paris. The only other evidence is the surviving religious embroideries, usually altered or cut up, where they remain in England, to meet changes in taste (Towneley Hall and Stonyhurst College, both Lancashire). *Opus anglicanum* was one of the glories of medieval England, coveted throughout Europe, where most of the examples remain. Otherwise we have to turn to illustrations to gain an idea of the emblazoned arms and crests on banners and hangings, bed draperies, the covering of furniture with silk and damask fabrics, and other items that brought colour and comfort to otherwise cold and cheerless rooms.

The one textile exception is *tapestries*, a development of the later fourteenth

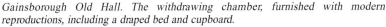

Gainsborough Old Hall. The withdrawing chamber, furnished with modern reproductions, including a draped bed and cupboard.

century that quickly became the most sought-after and expensive item in northern Europe. Designed as wall-hangings, they could be readily transported from house to house, increased the warmth and comfort of a domestic environment and created a sumptuous public or private setting that bespoke the wealth of the owner. The subjects included classical epics, chivalric romances, arms and heraldic devices, and stories from the Bible. Several late medieval sets survive in museums in New York, Paris, Angers and London, with the last holding four hunting tapestries of c.1425–30 that may have been commissioned by the first Earl of Shrewsbury (died 1453), from whom they passed to the sixth Earl (died 1590) and thence to his widow, who used them to furnish Hardwick Hall (Derbyshire). Heraldic tapestries blazoned with the owner's arms and badges continued the practice previously noted in stained glass and tiles. That with the royal arms decorating the hall dais at Haddon Hall is attributed to c.1460–70, while that at Nether Winchendon House carries the arms of Henry VIII. The tapestry of a mounted knight of c.1480 at Montacute House (Somerset) is an example of the figurative form in another medium, previously seen as a wall-painting at Penshurst Place. The tapestry of c.1500–10 in St Mary's Hall, Coventry, is the only one that has never been moved from its original high-table position. Tapestries could also be used to cover beds, tables, chairs and benches, particularly after they had become damaged or worn. For those unable to afford such hangings, painted cloths were a reasonable substitute. They had existed long before tapestries and continued to be made until the eighteenth century. Probate records show that they were common at all

Tattershall Castle, Lincolnshire. This second-floor chamber of Lord Cromwell's tower-house is hung with sixteenth-century Flemish tapestries, introduced in 1913. The chests are sixteenth-century while the oak table is dated 1586. The elaborate heraldic chimney-piece displays Lord Cromwell's coats of arms and the purse of the Treasurer of England.

Haddon Hall. The millefleur tapestry with the Garter-enclosed royal arms of England quartered with France is attributed to c.1460–70. Now highlighting the hall dais, it always seems to have been part of the house's furnishings. The table may be late fifteenth-century, and the panelling is seventeenth-century.

social levels, though only fragments survive from the Middle Ages, such as that with the arms of the Buxton family (*c.*1470) in the Strangers' Hall, Norwich. Probably the finest set is that of 1715 displayed at Owlpen Manor (Gloucestershire), illustrating the Prodigal Son and Joseph in vivid landscapes.

GARDENS

Gardens were integral to the layout and display of a house. Like furniture, they have been subject to centuries of change and fashion, so that no unaltered medieval garden survives. It is now appreciated that the moats widened on one or more sides of a castle to create small lakes were a deliberate landscaping feature enhancing the building's setting, as at Framlingham (Suffolk), Saltwood (Kent) and Kenilworth. Contemporary landscaping was integral to the approach at Bodiam and Bronsil castles, while the outer court of Whittington Castle (Shropshire) incorporated the earliest viewing mount discovered so far, set within an elaborate ditched water system. Lamphey Palace (Pembrokeshire) retains the cross-paths that created the quadrants of a late medieval garden, while the still visible fishponds were almost certainly ornamental. Medieval gardens have been recreated at Winchester Castle, Buckden Palace and Tretower Court, but the burgeoning discipline of garden archaeology will doubtless reveal more original survivals in a domestic context. The comparable discipline of landscape setting and estate development is also set to extend the

Buckden Palace, Cambridgeshire. The reconstruction of a medieval garden in the grounds of the palace, with the Bishop of Lincoln's residential brick tower of c.1472–85 in the background. The contemporary embattled wall conceals a raised walkway for viewing such a garden.

canvas of house development and expansion. This opens up the subject of land usage, estate management, financial investment and economic security or uncertainty on which so many secular houses depended. This is a field that has been little investigated so far, other than in relation to monastic institutions.

We are straying from the overview of house contents and furnishings to broader related subjects. The domestic items noted hint at a richly diverse resource that has been severely limited through deliberate destruction, changing taste, financial imperatives and fragility. Even so, what survives reveals that it is no longer necessary to consider English medieval art and artefacts as inferior to those in France. This is even clearer if ecclesiastical survivals are taken into account. Much English art reveals high-quality craftsmanship, creativity and taste, though England has its fair share of routine workmanship. While France was noted for ivories, manuscripts and gilded work, England was famous across Europe for textiles, misericords, pewter, funeral brasses, and alabasters. Nor was England insular, but deeply involved in a two-way market. England was as anxious to find outlets for its artistic craftsmanship as its wool and cloth products, while patrons sought the best craftsmen in a particular field, whether it be at home or abroad, as illustrated by the handful of early oil paintings that have survived in England. Unfortunately, little remains in an original domestic context, though there was a considerable expansion in known artefacts during the twentieth century. It is to be hoped that this practice of discovery will continue and thereby create an even broader corpus of medieval art, furniture and furnishings that demonstrate the diverse standards of secular patronage in England and Wales throughout the Middle Ages.

7. Medieval houses as a response to political circumstances: 1250-1450

Houses were frequently built or extended in response to political circumstances, usually the prospect of war or attack, but sometimes as a consequence of peace or a political settlement. They were also built or developed to make an authoritarian statement or as an assertion of political or military success. There is a correlation between these last two aspects, as will be illustrated by the consequences of the Hundred Years' War with France, but the factor of war and peace in house development has an extended history.

The Norman conquest of England was responsible for the wave of castle building – that assertion of an invading elite – essential for dominating the indigenous population. The mid-twelfth-century wars between Stephen and Matilda were responsible for many additional castles, while the 'new' castles of the thirteenth century were a consolidation of the aristocracy in England after the collapse of Angevin rule in northern France under King John. The close connection between politics and house development becomes particularly clear from the late thirteenth century in northern England and in Wales.

NORTHERN ENGLAND AND THE WAR AGAINST SCOTLAND

Good personal relations existed between the Scottish and English monarchs during the mid thirteenth century, contributing to the period of quiet prosperity that marked Northumbria until the close of the century. There were few castles in the region, while undefended seigneurial houses were fairly common. The majority were first-floor halls above substantial ground-floor chambers (usually a lesser hall), following the powerful episcopal precedents at Norham (Northumberland) and Durham castles, with several of them attaining considerable elegance towards the close of the century, as at Haughton (c.1260–80) and Edlingham (c.1300), both in Northumberland. They differed from superior houses in the Midlands and southern England by their narrowness, two-storey form and absence of aisled halls, but otherwise they followed the practice of offices and family chamber blocks at the lower and upper ends. They might have become an extremely popular form of considerable size and openness across northern England had not the political situation radically changed.

Edward I's obstinate claim in 1296 to be recognised *de facto* as overlord of the Scottish throne was followed by his intemperate invasion of Scotland. For the first few years, with nearly all the fighting on Scottish soil, victory seemed almost within his grasp. But a sequence of increasingly successful raids by Robert Bruce following Edward I's death in 1307 culminated in a Scottish victory at Bannockburn (1314). For the next eight years, Bruce led campaigns of terror across Northumberland and County Durham as well as Cumbria, northern and much of central Yorkshire until the independence of Scotland was recognised by the Treaty of Northampton (1328).

Until then, private fortification had been slow to develop and small in scale,

Aydon 'Castle', Northumberland. The initial development of 1296 at Aydon consisted of an upper and lower hall range with the upper hall reached by an external stair, formerly protected by a lean-to roof. The upper chamber block is to the left. This structure exemplifies the layout and comfortable standards of minor gentry during Edward I's reign.

but a series of costly campaigns in the mid 1330s by Edward III gave heart to the people of northern England. Scottish defeat and the capture of David Bruce

at Neville's Cross near Durham (1346) encouraged a more assertive building response at grass-root level. The change can be followed by comparing the form and development of Aydon Hall with that of Belsay Castle (both in Northumberland). Aydon was developed by Robert Reymes, a wealthy merchant who left Suffolk in about 1296 to build a retirement home in the Tyne valley. He followed the local practice of developing both floors as hall and chamber blocks with the more important and elegant apartments on

Aydon 'Castle'. One of the late thirteenth-century twin-light windows of the chamber block. The carved head, possibly God the Father, was carved for a chapel that was never realised. The infilled holes once held iron grilles.

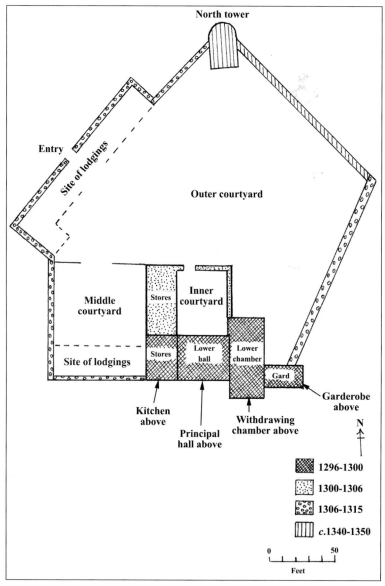

Aydon 'Castle': ground plan.

the upper floor, as was the all-important kitchen. At first the invasions were all towards Scotland but, with the reversal in fortune, Scottish incursions made defence essential. A second kitchen block was added to serve a possible garrison and a battlemented courtyard was added to the front (1305–6) but it was subsequently necessary to add an enclosing curtain wall (by 1315) and a semicircular tower (by *c.*1350). As northern England knew little respite from

97

Aydon 'Castle'. Ten years later, Robert Reymes erected a two-storey kitchen wing (centre) against the lower end of the hall, now marked by the gable outline of a lost lodging range. He also erected the embattled wall with entry that created the small courtyard in front of the hall.

Scottish attacks throughout Edward II's weak rule, little building activity was undertaken until the tide began to turn in England's favour. Then an era of house building was initiated that continued until the early years of the next century.

The quadrangular form was favoured at first by the more wealthy knights, consisting of a rectangular enclosure with curtain walls, angle towers, a plain entrance, and one or more residential ranges against the curtain, as at Ford (1338) and

Aydon 'Castle'. The external face of the kitchen and hall block showing the superb chimney stack serving the lower hall fireplace. It illustrates the refined living standards of c.1300 in a border house, as do the uppermost windows.

Langley Castle, Northumberland. After Warkworth, this is the most complex of the Northumbrian tower-houses. It was built shortly after 1346 by Sir Thomas Lucy, a survivor of Crécy and principal commander at the Battle of Neville's Cross near Durham. His house is a bravura statement of regional standing, wealth and aspiration.

Chillingham (1344). They were the precursors of the plan adopted by the next generation, who integrated the courtyard ranges and angle towers in a unified concept with dominating corner towers, as at Danby (Yorkshire, *c*.1370), and Lumley (1390s). For most landed families in the region, more compact and cheaper single towers proved popular, with Etal (1341), leading the way, followed by Langley (*c*.1340–60) and Edlingham (*c*.1350–60), all in Northumberland. Increasingly extended periods of peace brought their proliferation, including Belsay (*c*.1370–80), Chipchase (*c*.1380), not far away, and Ayton (Yorkshire, 1390–1400). The fact that large numbers were erected across the whole of the northern region was a recognition that vigilance was essential in the face of ongoing insecurity and uncertainty.

Virtually all northern residences built between 1300 and 1550 were defensive, but, no matter how strong externally, they primarily fulfilled a domestic purpose – family occupation. They took one of two forms. The more extensive group was austere solar towers, usually three-storeyed, consisting of ground-floor storage, a withdrawing chamber above, with the retiring chamber

Belsay Castle, Northumberland. This is one of the most compact and impressive tower-houses in Northumberland. It is basically a tautly planned three-storey structure with a single chamber on each floor – kitchen, hall and withdrawing chamber respectively. Built in c.1370–80, the lower part of the entrance front was covered in 1614 by a multi-windowed manor house (left), now ruined.

Belsay Castle. Built of large blocks of locally quarried sandstone, the sheer walls of this tower-house terminate in a defensive superstructure of boldly projecting rounded bartisans and machicolated battlemented parapets. Compared with the open and relaxed domestic scale of Aydon, tower-houses like Belsay were more tautly planned and much easier to defend.

on the uppermost floor, all newel-linked internally. The tower was usually attached to the upper end of a hall, as at Edlingham, Halton and Shortflatt (all in Northumberland), so that the tower could become a self-contained refuge in times of danger. The halls were frequently of wood, so that many towers survive when the hall and offices have been lost or replaced, as at Belsay and Shortflatt. Belsay is one of the more elaborate of these solar towers, with generously scaled chambers, additional private rooms in the thickened west wall, mid-fifteenth-century wall-paintings in the first-floor withdrawing chamber, and a roof crowned with tall battlemented parapets, corner turrets and machicolations. A few years after the unification of England and Scotland (1603) brought an era of relative peace, the possible site of an early great hall was replaced by a more comfortable house, which is now ruined.

The second group of towers were larger, more complex and entirely free-standing. Entry was usually at ground level, with the kitchen and offices nearby, the hall at first-floor level, with the retiring chamber above. Built by lesser magnates as well as knights, Langley (c.1340–60), Gilling (Yorkshire, c.1360–80), Haughton after heightening (c.1370) and Hylton (1390–1405) are particularly fine examples with elaborate windows and a commanding heraldic display above the entrance at Hylton.

Over 160 towered houses were built in Northumberland between 1340 and 1550 and about 120 in Cumbria. However, there are only twenty-seven in Yorkshire, ten in County Durham and a scatter in Lancashire, reflecting the lack of Scottish penetration southwards after the battle of Neville's Cross. The size and scale of these towers, built as a necessary defence against sudden raids rather than sieges, also made a statement about the standing of the owners, just as the magnate tower-houses did at Warkworth and Alnwick castles. And if the

Alnwick Castle, Northumberland. Compared with the towers of knights at Belsay and Langley, Lord Percy's early to mid fourteenth-century keep and gatehouse were intended to be a major bastion defending the border with Scotland. Percy initiated and his son completed the reforming of the earlier shell keep by the addition of seven D-shaped towers, prefaced by the remodelled entrance gateway. The reconstruction was a military necessity, but the apartments were on a scale that suggests a prototype palace-fortress.

form was dictated by political events, they quickly became permanent homes. They cost too much to build, the rooms were too useful and they developed an element of comfort that makes many of them still satisfactory for residential use today (Langley; Mortham Tower; Shortflatt).

There was far less building activity in northern England during the fifteenth century than the fourteenth. This was principally because all the leading families had equipped themselves with the necessary defensive elements to make their homes secure. The border also became less susceptible to Scottish attacks as a consequence of several ineffective monarchs and a Scottish nobility who were more concerned with factious self-interests than attacking the enemy south of the border. There were intermittent attempts to engage with the English (1456–7, 1481–3) but otherwise there was little more than local skirmishes that degenerated into large-scale cattle thieving on either side of the border. In addition, the period from the late 1430s to the 1470s was one of economic recession, reduced income and empty holdings. Though this crisis affected much of the country, its impact was felt far more harshly in the north than in the Midlands or southern England. This bleakness is reflected in the lack of domestic development. A residential gatehouse at Bywell (Northumberland), and remodelled family accommodation at Warkworth further north, and that at Penrith and Appleby castles (both Cumbria) was the sum of magnate activity in those counties, while modest towers continued to be erected by minor landowners, as at Cockle Park (1461–9) and Hefferlaw (after 1470) in Northumberland. In contrast, the majority of towers in Yorkshire were of solar

Middleton Hall, Cumbria. This late fourteenth-century hall and cross-wing house of the Middleton family in Cumbria was protected by an almost contemporary defensive wall. It stands about 18 feet (5.5 metres) high to the embattled wall walk, with a two-storey gatehouse and end towers.

Nappa Hall, Yorkshire. The Metcalfe family of Nappa Hall was one of modest means until the fortunes of Thomas Metcalfe multiplied in the service of Richard, Duke of Gloucester (later Richard III), of nearby Middleham Castle. Thomas was responsible for the central hall, flanked at each end by a tower, with that at the upper end being of four storeys. Its lack of defensive intent is made clear by the window size, which is in reverse order to the usual form.

form, mainly erected during the fifteenth century. They had more windows and were more lightly defended, as at Crayke, Hellifield, Paull Holme and Nappa Hall, this last the only house to have retained its original hall and offices (1470–80). But the wars between Scotland and England were not so much brought to an end by truce or peace as by a *coup de grâce* at Flodden Field (1513), when the attempt to take advantage of the absence of English military forces abroad ended in a catastrophic failure for the Scottish king, his death on the battlefield, and the elimination of a large proportion of the Scottish nobility.

THE CONQUEST OF WALES

The mountainous mass of the Welsh heartland had confined the Anglo-Norman conquest of Wales between c.1070 and 1170 to the hilly borderland stretching from Chester to Chepstow and to the coastal lowland of south Wales, with limited penetration along the narrow north coast. By the close of the twelfth century Wales was a country of two peoples – the Welsh and the Anglo-Normans. They were marked by totally different social and economic systems – the former by clans and divided holdings on death, the latter by lordships, the manorial system and primogeniture. Anglo-Norman occupation introduced tightly planned two-storey stone houses with the family rooms above vaulted undercrofts. Over sixty examples have been identified so far, mainly in

Pembrokeshire (Eastington, Monkton Hall) but also in south Carmarthenshire (Penallt) and south Glamorgan (Castle Farm, St George-super-Ely), with the earliest attributed to the thirteenth century. That was also a period of virtual independence in central and north Wales under Llywelyn ap Iorwerth (1194–1240) and his grandson Llywelyn ap Gruffudd (1247–82). The latter, in particular, stemmed the tide of further English advance and forged a measure of unity and purpose throughout native Wales.

Ap Gruffudd's success spurred Edward I to crush all native resistance and impose the rule of English law. Success in the two wars of 1276–7 and 1282–3 determined the pattern of Welsh politics, administration and social structure for the next two hundred and fifty years. To help realise his plans, Edward inaugurated a campaign of fortress building of such magnitude – eight royal works supported by seven baronial castles – that all resistance was stifled. Several of these castles were built in association with fortified towns capable of protecting the newly arrived English traders and administration (Caernarfon, Conwy, Denbigh). The sudden introduction of alien practices, resources and people – some of whom settled locally – to build this concentration of works between 1277 and 1330 had a major impact on local building practices and a profound effect on the development of native Welsh houses.

These political circumstances meant that residential development in Wales was quite distinct from that in England. Castles were far more widespread during the twelfth and thirteenth centuries and tended to be lordship-held and occupied throughout the Middle Ages. Fortified towers and defensive houses were comparatively rare, that of de la Bere family at Weobley in the Gower peninsula (1304–27) being the most complete survival. Late medieval domestic

Cochwillan, Gwynedd. Looking towards Anglesey, this house was probably erected by Gruffudd ap Robin shortly after he had been appointed sheriff of Caernarvonshire in 1485 as a reward for supporting Henry VII at Bosworth Field. The hall is distinguished by the wall fireplace, a dais with canopy evidence, a hammer-beam roof, and high-quality woodwork.

Tretower Castle, Powys. This twelfth-century stone castle, with its more comfortable thirteenth-century round keep within it, was built in the valley of the river Usk by the Picard family. The castle was garrisoned against Glyn Dŵr's forces in 1403 but it was superseded shortly afterwards by the courtyard house built 200 yards away. This transition graphically illustrates the vital change from the defensive to a more peaceful era.

residences were usually smaller than in England, with the cruck truss form of construction particularly popular (Plas-ucha, Corwen c.1435; Ty-mawr, Castell Caereinion, c.1460). The timber-framed practices of Lancashire, Cheshire and Shropshire percolated the north-east during the fifteenth and early sixteenth centuries through spere trusses (Penarth-fawr, Pwllheli, c.1476), ornate screens, and a group of hammer-beam roofs (Cochwillan, Bethesda, 1480s). The proximity of the west Midlands and Herefordshire to the border affected the planning and decorative standards of houses, particularly the introduction of box-frame halls in Powys (Bryndraenog, c.1436) and the quadrangular concept (Tretower, 1450–80). Meanwhile, the early development of Anglo-Norman stone

Tretower Court, Powys. The home of Sir Roger Vaughan, the Court developed in a sequence of phases beginning shortly before 1450. The hall in the centre is flanked by the services and kitchen (right, with seventeenth-century windows) and the private apartments to the left. Tretower is the grandest gentry house of late medieval Wales.

Tretower Court. The house was built round a courtyard. The upper half of the ground-floor hall of 1447 was probably timber-framed, but it was rebuilt in stone in the seventeenth century, when the present doorway and windows were inserted. The stone bay window was a late fifteenth-century insertion in the withdrawing room, while the first-floor guest chambers in the north range were entered from the projecting timber-framed gallery (1450–80).

St David's Palace, Pembrokeshire. One of the best-preserved episcopal palaces in England or Wales as a consequence of its abandonment in 1542. Much of it is by a particularly enthusiastic building bishop, Henry Gower (1328–47). He began by erecting a first-floor hall (left) and chamber block for his personal use, crowned by the distinctive arcaded parapet that was the hall-mark of his work. In a second phase, he built a magnificent ceremonial hall (right), approached through an ornate porch. Both halls were linked in a third phase by a new kitchen in the angle of the two halls, served by a corridor (centre) and the porch added to the private hall.

houses in the far south had culminated in Bishop Gower's mid-fourteenth-century expansion of his palaces at St David's and Lamphey to a scale and standard comparable with those of many English sees.

Architectural historians have tended to underestimate the vast damage that was a consequence of Owain Glyn Dŵr's rebellion against English authority between 1400 and 1410. As Glyn Dŵr's purpose was to destroy all centres of alien power and control, more castles and towns were besieged, captured or damaged during Henry IV's reign than at any other time in England or Wales throughout the later Middle Ages. Many ecclesiastical palaces and monasteries were fired and ravaged, while Glyn Dŵr's scorched-earth policy brought wholesale destruction to houses and lesser dwellings throughout most of Wales, compounded by the devastation of retaliating English troops. Unlike many popular insurrections, this rebellion was a national rising, not limited to one particular stratum of society. It was a major drain on Henry IV's financial resources and initiated an era of hardship in Wales that lasted for at least a generation. The consequence was that no timber-framed houses in Wales have been found that pre-date 1430. Throughout the remainder of the century, though, there was a substantial rebuilding programme, recently traced in detail in the timber-building county of Radnorshire.

8. Medieval houses as a response to political circumstances: 1330-1500

Whereas the wars with Scotland and Wales brought about fundamental changes in house development throughout northern England and Wales, two further conflicts – the Hundred Years' War and the Wars of the Roses – had more limited consequences, though the attenuated conflict with France affected a broad span of people.

THE HUNDRED YEARS' WAR

The Hundred Years' War is a convenient term to describe the struggle for supremacy between England and France that extended beyond the traditional limits of the 116 years from 1337 to 1453. It was not a continuous war but a series of vicious conflicts separated by extended periods of uneasy peace. Nor

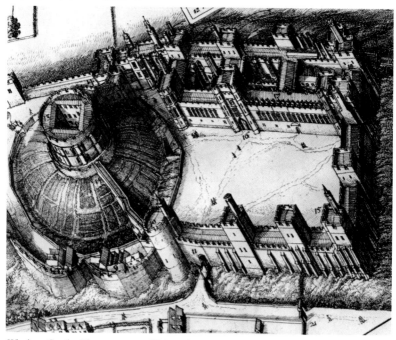

Windsor Castle. The sequence of Edward III's successes against the French during the first phase of the Hundred Years' War made him a king of European standing. The upper court of Windsor Castle was rebuilt to reflect his prestige and triumphant position as acclaimed head of the English nation. His work of 1353–70, shown here in Hollar's engraving of 1659, was radically altered by Charles II and George IV so that the architectural importance and significant consequences of Edward's palace-fortress have only been appreciated since some of his structures were revealed by fire in 1992.

was it limited to the Plantagenet and Valois dynasties but it involved the rulers of Brittany, Flanders, and Burgundy as well as those of Castile, Navarre, Portugal, and Scotland.

The gradual sequence of English successes during the first phase of the war from 1337 to 1360 brought an abundance of rewards. Some were immediate, like the visible trophies of conflict – French wall-hangings, gold plate, jewels and silk cloths. There was pardonable exaggeration in the claim by Thomas Walsingham that Edward III's campaign of 1346–7 meant that every woman in England enjoyed the pickings of Caen, Calais and other French towns for their 'coats, furs, quilts and household goods of every kind, table cloths, necklaces, wooden bowls and silver goblets, linen and cloth'. Yet numerous French items recorded in English inventories and wills over the next hundred years support the basis of the chronicler's comment. Other returns were more substantial and enduring, particularly those from capturing prized prisoners. Their ransoms funded the Duke of Lancaster's construction of the Savoy Palace in London at a cost of 52,000 marks (c.1350, destroyed), the Black Prince's Palace at Kennington in south London (1340–63, destroyed), and Edward III's extensive residential development of Windsor Castle (1352–77). But prowess on the battlefield also brought fame, peer-group esteem and a higher standing in society than before, which was frequently reflected in a new residence, such as those of William Clinton at Maxstoke (1342–6), and Sir John Norwich at Mettingham (Suffolk, 1343–50), or in major additions such as the tower-houses at Stafford and Beverston castles. Entrepreneurs also took advantage of the conflict to make a profit through servicing its needs. Commoners such as John Pulteney and William de la Pole became rich through lending money to the king, were knighted, and displayed their newly acquired respectability by building Penshurst Place (1341–9), and Suffolk Palace in Hull (1340–60, destroyed).

The third phase of the war, from 1415 to 1429, was equally rewarding but by this time the earlier scorched-earth policy practised across France had been replaced by the more efficient one of land settlement based on confiscated estates. It was the financial return from such holdings and their offices that funded Sir John Fastolf's castle at Caister (1437–55), while a number of returning soldiers, captains of war rather than magnates, developed new houses, including Ampthill (Bedfordshire, 1420s, destroyed), Hampton Court near Leominster (1434–47), and Rye House (1443). Even the reversal in English fortunes during the last phase of the war to 1453 failed to stem the wave of building activity, which included Stourton House (1430–40, destroyed), and Sudeley Castle (1441–58), both attributed by the Tudor chronicler John Leland 'to the spoils taken during the war with France'.

England was extremely fortunate that none of the fighting took place on English soil. Most of it occurred in France with some smaller fields of war in Spain, Portugal and Flanders. It is for this reason that far fewer medieval houses have survived in rural France than in England. Yet there were several occasions when the threat of attack along the southern coast became a reality. There were raids against Portsmouth and Southampton in 1338, Dover and Hastings in 1339, and Rye and Winchelsea in 1360. The Treaty of Brétigny in that year did not bring the hoped-for peace between the two countries. In fact, it was the second phase of the war that gave the French crown the opportunity to re-order its forces and prepare for the invasion of England.

The vulnerability of London to French naval attacks had persuaded Edward III to remodel Hadleigh Castle (Essex, 1360s), and build Queenborough Castle, (Kent, 1370s, destroyed), to help protect the Thames estuary. French raids against the vulnerable south-east towns became all too real by the late 1370s so that panic measures, embracing royal, civic and private enterprise, started to be taken from 1378 until at least 1392. This was a time when the architectural distinction between defence and modest protection and between private and more public schemes was blurred. The king rebuilt the keep at Southampton Castle, heightened the gatehouse at Carisbrooke Castle (Isle of Wight), strengthened Rochester Castle, and put the other royal castles on a state of alert (1378–83). Several leading magnates supported this activity. Lord Cobham built Cooling Castle (Kent, 1380), Archbishop Courtenay erected an impressive gatehouse and towered outer bailey at Saltwood (1382–5), while Bishop Wykeham helped to wall the city of Winchester and his palace there. Private landowners similarly sought to protect their properties, not as part of any concerted scheme but as an individual reaction to the anticipated foreign invasion. The fortified houses in Kent at Scotney (1378) and Hever (1383) were essentially new works by local gentry while the earlier house of Lord St John at Halnaker, and the Bishop of Chichester's house at Amberley, both in Sussex, were given the protection of towered walls and gatehouses (c.1377–82).

The possibility of a Franco-Burgundian invasion became a frightening probability in 1385, the year in which Sir Edward Dalyngrigge was granted a

Amberley Castle, Sussex. The manor house of the Bishops of Chichester was converted into a castle by Bishop Rede, who erected the gatehouse and curtain walls under a licence to crenellate in December 1377. The lack of projecting towers at the angles of the enclosure and midway along the curtain, the construction of a dry moat, and the absence of machicolations and a drawbridge suggest that defensive strength was secondary to speedy completion.

110

Halnaker House, Sussex. Another example where a manor house near Chichester was defended in the late 1370s. Built of flint rubble, the gatehouse of the defensive frontage was flanked by a projecting angle tower (left). However, advantage was taken of the situation to develop high-quality residential accommodation immediately behind this frontage.

licence 'to make into a castle his manor house at Bodiam near the sea'. Why the French abandoned the invasion is unclear, but though the scare gradually diminished, particularly after a three-year truce in 1389, protective building activity continued. The crown repaired the decayed keep at Canterbury and the civic authorities at Canterbury and Winchester pressed on with their defensive work programmes, while private construction continued, with Sir John Devereux fortifying his entirely domestic residence at Penshurst (1392). The

Penshurst Place, Kent. In 1392 Sir John Devereux was granted a licence to enclose and tower his manor house at Penshurst. The earlier house was encircled with an embattled wall, defended by three-storey towers at the corners and lesser towers in the middle of each side. Only the isolated garden tower remains complete (right), though some of the other towers and walling have been incorporated in the later development of the house.

threat of invasion receded when a relatively permanent truce was signed in 1396, bringing to a close the most extensive spate of defensive building activity between Edward I's subjugation of Wales and Henry VIII's defence of the south coast against French attack in the late 1530s.

The threat of enemy invasion was met by differing responses in architectural and defensive terms. Queenborough Castle, the only royal one built on a fresh site throughout the later Middle Ages, was of concentric circular design with a central 'rotunda'. Cooling Castle was a hastily built defensive station with a substantial outer ward capable of holding large numbers of troops, as was the case at Saltwood Castle. These were serious defences, but though Sir Edward Dalyngrigge took the opportunity to build an imposing structure at Bodiam that seemed to promise serious defence, it was primarily a show castle in a landscaped setting. These castles are among the earliest exemplars in England to deploy artillery through circular and keyhole-shaped gunports but, while Bodiam and Cooling adopted particularly wide moats, Saltwood and to a lesser extent Scotney made a feature of more extensive water defences.

Nor were these years without their effect on domestic houses in south-east England. Hever adopted the towered rectangular plan of Bodiam, while the residential core of Halnaker was protected by a formidable frontage. The two courts at Scotney were an adaptation of the Cooling design to another lowland site, while the earlier houses at Amberley and Penshurst were now enclosed by high perimeter walls and towers. The decision to build defensively was particularly likely with war veterans such as Cobham, Dalyngrigge and Lord St John who had experienced the tension, fear and material destruction of invading forces when they were abroad. Their houses may have been out of the imminent reach of short-lived attacks, but their owner's reaction to the prospect of invasion was just as immediate as the sea-facing fortresses of an earlier generation at Dover, Pevensey, and Portchester.

THE WARS OF THE ROSES

The sequence of wars and campaigns between about 1452 and 1487 known collectively as the Wars of the Roses was not a broad-based civil strife like the Peasants' Revolt of 1381 but a political rift between the ruling house of Lancaster (via Edward III's third son, John of Gaunt, Duke of Lancaster) and supporters of the house of York (via Edward III's second son, Lionel, through marriage and descent to the reforming Duke of York). The wars were a series of short-lived conflicts separated by extended phases of peace over a thirty-five year period. They were marked by extraordinary reversals of fortune for the protagonists but affected few outside the crown, the greater nobility and their supporters. Pillaging or destruction were rare, while many parts of England never even saw an army. Unlike Glyn Dŵr's revolt, hardly any towns were attacked, apart from London (1471). Few castles were besieged, other than the French-supported dissidents encased in Harlech and Denbigh in north Wales and those with the former queen in Alnwick and Bamburgh in Northumberland. The destruction of Belvoir Castle (1461), and the damage to Gainsborough Old Hall (1470), during the wars were essentially the consequence of local politics.

Unlike the Hundred Years' War, the conflict brought no rush to develop new fortresses or add defences to existing residences except in one particular instance. Between 1445 and 1485 a group of independent tower-houses was erected, all by Yorkist leaders or supporters, defensive in purpose and intended to protect the Yorkist hegemony from its Lancastrian enemies. Those at Raglan and Ashby de la Zouch still stand to roof level, while the lower walls and foundations of those at Warwick and Hunsdon can still be traced. No comparable Lancastrian structures were necessary when they were protected by such well-maintained fortresses as Middleham, Richmond, Tutbury and Kenilworth castles. Yet the political and personal failure of these four Yorkist tower-houses marks the final sundering of the architectural cloth that had bound fortification and domestic comfort in harmony for the previous two centuries.

When Richard, Duke of York, came of age in 1432 he was the richest landowner in England and a magnate of royal blood. As he opposed the peace policy with France advocated by the ineffective Henry VI during the closing stages of the Hundred Years' War, he was sent away to Ireland in 1447 in a clumsy attempt to banish him from the political scene. By treating the Duke as the enemy, the King and his supporters turned him into one. The licence which the Duke received in 1447 to crenellate his house at Hunsdon in Hertfordshire specifically mentions a tower of stone. What was built there was in brick (cheaper and quicker than stone), begun over a year earlier, probably stood five storeys high, was separately moated and positioned within a defendable precinct. Only its partial foundations and some walls incorporated into a Regency house reveal the massive scale of this tower-house, which cost 7,000 marks (£4,667) to build. It also served as the Duke's base not far from London after his unexpected return from Ireland in 1450 and throughout his ruthless pursuit of reform against the King's 'evil councillors' and his claim to the throne in 1460 until his death on the battlefield two months later.

Hunsdon House, Hertfordshire. The present brick residence of 1805–10 incorporates part of the fifteenth-century brick tower-house initiated by Richard, Duke of York, in 1446. Part of the tower's foundations was revealed in 1983, including this base of the gateway turret. The tower was almost as large as that at Tattershall Castle (page 132) but was more obviously of military intent.

Raglan Castle, Monmouthshire. The tower-house at Raglan is likely to have been raised in about 1460 to secure the Yorkist victory in Wales. It has lost its uppermost floor and the machicolated parapet as seen on the entry tower to the rear.

The second tower was developed at about this time by the passionate Yorkist supporter Sir William Herbert at Raglan, probably shortly after York's son Edward won the throne in 1461. Edward IV needed to crush any Lancastrian resistance to his rule and did so by appointing faithful supporters to key posts in different parts of the country. At first it looked as though the Earl of Warwick, who already held Cardiff Castle, was going to be given responsibility in Wales but at the last minute the task was put into Herbert's hands. The tower-house he built not only consolidated Herbert's virtually viceregal position in Wales but also gave him protection from the neighbour who became his ruthless enemy and nemesis, Warwick the Kingmaker. The Raglan tower was five-storeyed, elaborately defended externally, with tiered apartments, including a kitchen with its own

Raglan Castle. Shortly before his creation as Earl of Pembroke in 1468, Sir William Herbert had erected the highly impressive entrance on the west side of the castle, flanked by an imposing residential range (left) and the corner tower for guests (right). Even in its ruined state, the extensive remains of Raglan testify to the dramatic rise of a Welsh border family to a position of power, leadership and domestic magnificence.

Ashby de la Zouch Castle, Leicestershire. William, Lord Hastings, erected this tower-house between the licence of 1474, and 1480 when he turned his attention to rebuilding the family home at Kirby Muxloe. The low entrance gave access to a dark lobby and stair, with the remainder of the ground floor serving as a staff hall. Above were the first-floor kitchen with a vaulted ceiling, the audience chamber, and Hastings's with-drawing chamber with its magnificent fireplace. There was a sequence of seven subsidiary rooms in the turret to the right.

Ashby de la Zouch Castle. As part of his expansion of the earlier manor, Lord Hastings built this particularly spacious family chapel, lit by nine generous windows. It was flanked by a two-storey residential range (right), which continued round two further sides of the small chapel court (see plan on pages 58-9).

fresh water supply, and a dominating position within the castle as the place of last resort for the Herbert family.

The third tower-house was constructed shortly after Edward IV's return to the throne in 1471 by Sir William Hastings, charged by the King with crushing dissident Lancastrian revolt in the Midlands from his power-base at Ashby de la Zouch. Converting his long-established manor house into a more defendable residence, Hastings erected a tower-house in about 1474 that included portcullis and machicolations but was more clearly intended for regular residential use with a rising sequence of highly decorative and imposing apartments. (Not long afterwards, Edward IV also added a substantial residential tower at Nottingham Castle that similarly possessed a defensive capability, though linked to a multi-windowed apartment range.)

Edward's death in 1483 was shortly followed by that of his great friend Hastings, who, like Herbert, was beheaded without trial. The newly crowned king, Richard III, sought to consolidate Yorkist rule against a rising tide of enemies. A more competent soldier than most of his contemporaries, Richard chose Warwick Castle as one of his centres of operation, partly because the Midlands was a region of Lancastrian sympathy, but also because a recent rebellion had shown him the benefit of a central control point for moving troops quickly to different parts of the country. The new king began constructing his tower-house on the side of Warwick Castle facing the town, but independent of all other buildings within the castle's circuit. It was larger than Lord Cromwell's brick tower-house at Tattershall but similar in proportion and scale to that at Hunsdon. But Richard III was killed at the battle of Bosworth Field before the

Warwick Castle. Buck's engraving of 1729 shows the lower part of the massive tower-house (centre and right) raised by Richard III. Probably incomplete at the time of his death on the battlefield in 1485, the tower was reduced to first-floor level and the inner half destroyed in the early seventeenth century. When completed, it would have been substantially larger than that at Tattershall.

structure could be completed, so that only its two mutilated lower storeys survive, the so-called Clarence and Bear towers.

With the accession of Henry VII in 1485 and his policy of reconciliation, the Wars of the Roses spluttered to a close. Each of these tower-houses had been built by a supporter of the house of York to help consolidate and protect its rule. Independent of other structures, externally formidable but inwardly comfortable, none of them saved its owner from sudden death nor in any way delayed the advent of the calmer days that gradually unfurled under Tudor rule. The thread that had long joined fortification and domestic comfort was finally broken as the fresh winds of the Renaissance flowed through the increasingly open windows of English houses.

Compton Castle. As a result of French coastal raids and piratical attacks, particularly after the English defeat in the Hundred Years' War, the fourteenth-century manor house at Compton was fortified with a defensive frontage that included machicolations, gunports, portcullises and four added towers. It was built between 1450 and 1480, when the nearby castles at Berry Pomeroy and Dartmouth were also militarily developed.

9. Medieval houses as an expression of social status

Houses of any era reflect the spread of wealth, the rise of new families, social differentiation and the development of household institutions. Though the homes of medieval merchant, yeoman, and peasant society have their own significant interest, much of the thrust of architectural study during the later Middle Ages lies in the development of the domestic residences and households of the crown, aristocracy and gentry. For what they achieved at national, regional and local levels affected the government, the economy, the welfare and the social justice or injustice of the country throughout all levels of contemporary society. They also determined the character, the taste and the standards of that society, and their houses are the visible witness to those standards. Each of those buildings tells us much about the status of its builder. It can indicate, for instance, the size of his patrimony, his financial resources, his political standing and the scale of his household. For a house is a living organism. It expresses the needs, the habits, the energy, the taste and the imagination of its builder and his descendants. Most houses, of course, are subject to the changes and modifications of later generations, but in distinguishing those changes one can also see the aspirations and culture of later generations – whether they are of the fifteenth, the seventeenth or the nineteenth centuries.

THE HOUSEHOLD

With the gradual reduction in the number of properties held by the leaders of society during the fourteenth century, the crown and aristocracy concentrated their resources on those that mattered, expanding and improving the comfort of the residences that they favoured. And in so doing they also helped to build up their sphere of influence – their 'locality'. That of John of Gaunt was centred on Leicester and Kenilworth castles in the Midlands, and to a lesser extent at Tutbury and Higham Ferrers, not far away. He also enjoyed visiting and updated Pontefract Castle, in the centre of his northern estates, and expanded Hertford Castle, at the heart of his south-eastern interests. In the mid fifteenth century Richard, Duke of York, had extensive estates on the Welsh border based on Wigmore and Ludlow castles, with further centres of locality in Northamptonshire (Fotheringhay Castle), Yorkshire (Sandal Castle), eastern England (Clare and Stamford castles) and the pale in Ireland (Trim Castle).

Just as each great magnate had his 'locality', so did each rank below – from lesser magnate, knight banneret and knight, down to esquire. The more important of them would have several houses, like the Berkeley family who dominated Gloucestershire from their *caput* at Berkeley Castle, supported by relations with castles at Beverston and Dursley, the defensive houses at Coberley and Yate, and the manor house at Wotton-under-Edge. Most knights had to be satisfied with one or two houses of quality, but they shared the same outlook, aspirations and values in life as a magnate and therefore emulated those of high rank in their standards of living, the form of their household, and the scale of their houses.

Beverston Castle, Gloucestershire. The early thirteenth-century castle was extended shortly after its purchase by Thomas, Lord Berkeley, in 1330, when he added the dominating rectangular tower next to the earlier hall range. Internally complex, the apartments include two chapels – jewels of that period. This residential tower should be compared with its near contemporaries at Stokesay and South Kyme. The former moat has been incorporated in the landscaping of the still-occupied house.

It is often forgotten that houses are essentially an envelope to contain a household, whether a magnificent one or that of a modest family. Furthermore, we know considerably more about the form and development of the medieval house than we do about the medieval household. Yet the size, splendour and hospitality of a medieval household were an indication of a lord's standing in society. It expressed his 'lordship' and, in so doing, made a political statement. The scale and magnificence of a medieval household made an equally important social statement in which display and ceremony contributed even more than hospitality and charity. It is important to have an idea of how many people we are discussing. In very broad brushstrokes, the upper ranks of late medieval society encompassed a diminishing number of peers, shrinking from about 150 members in 1350 to about 70 in 1450, made up of a dozen or so dukes and earls and between forty and fifty magnates. During the same period the number of knights seems to have fallen from about 1,100 to nearly 700, not as a result of declining income but as a consequence of greater selectivity. The esquires, who began as a chivalric class but increasingly became involved in local government during the fifteenth century, possibly numbered between about 800 and 1,200 members, with the lower number applicable towards the accession of the Tudors. It is these three strata of society who held or sought to establish major houses and filled them with a household that reflected their 'estate' – their rank, their public standing and their generosity. It should be borne in mind, though, that even during the later Middle Ages buildings were used as an expression of status considerably further down the social scale.

A household was almost entirely a male society throughout our period. The only women were washerwomen, a nurse for the householder's children, and the serving ladies of the lord's wife. The situation started to change among the lower ranks of a household during the later fifteenth century, but throughout our period wives and children were expected to live outside or away from the employer's residence. The largest household was that of the king, which rose in number from about 350 to 380 staff under Edward II and to about 800 during the reign of Henry VI. But some research on the food consumption of magnate families suggests that the largest households occurred during the first half of the fourteenth century and that they decreased during the late fourteenth and fifteenth centuries, when they numbered between 100 and 200 people, with an upsurge towards the close of the century.

A household was a very hierarchical organisation, with clearly defined departments, responsibilities and status rules. It was divided into two groups – those permanently attached to a house, and those who were only periodically associated with it. The *permanent* household included the chief officers: the steward accountable for the conduct and day-to-day running of the household, the chamberlain responsible for the lord's private chambers, and the treasurer. Lower down the social scale would be the cook, responsible for running the kitchen – and one of the highest paid employees in the household. Under him would be the pantler supervising the bread and table linen, and the butler controlling the ale, beer and wine. The wardrober took charge of the lord's clothes, jewels, furniture and furnishings, while the marshal accounted for the stables, grooms and transport arrangements. Those who were *occasional* members of the household included estate administrators, bailiffs, reeves, auditors and lawyers. Indentured retainers, despite the extensive literature about them, seem to have been unusual, while the wearing of livery was standard.

The nobility and gentry not only shared the same attitudes, lifestyle and aspirations, but there was little distinction between their homes either. There is no obvious differentiation in the size and character of the magnate's house at Wingfield in Derbyshire (1439–56) and the knight's house nearby at Haddon Hall (*c.*1330–50, extended

Wingfield Manor, Derbyshire. The hall porch and one of the residential ranges of Lord Cromwell's commanding mansion. Directly opposite the starker inner gateway, their enriched treatment deliberately heightened the approach to the ceremonial hall and Cromwell's more personal apartments.

Wingfield Manor. The interior of the hall looking towards the cross-passage, not unlike that of the Bishop's Palace at Lincoln built over two hundred years earlier. Between the entry porch (left) and the triple service doorways was a washing recess. The gable window illuminated the roof while the side walls below the windows were covered with wall-hangings or tapestries.

Wingfield Manor. The vaulted undercroft directly below the hall was occupied by staff. Doors in each corner facilitated their rapid attendance on the lord and his family. The building account for 1443 refers to the construction of a vaulted chamber of comparable size.

Oxburgh Hall, Norfolk. The licence granted to Sir Edmund Bedingfield in 1482 to crenellate his house at Oxburgh is still preserved there. Its wording suggests that building may have already begun as it forgives Sir Edmund for any constructions previously made. The gatehouse stands complete and untouched, but most of the two-storeyed ranges round the courtyard were remodelled during the eighteenth and nineteenth centuries (particularly the windows and internal fittings), while the south-west tower (right) is a Victorian concoction on the site of the original kitchen.

between 1425 and 1500). West Bromwich Manor House with its impressive hall was built by a Staffordshire squire, Richard Marnham, in *c.*1275, whereas the modest residential block of 1305 not far away at Norbury was that of the wealthy knight Sir Henry Fitzherbert. Though the defendable house at Caister was built by Sir John Fastolf (1432–45), the standard of accommodation and its luxurious appointments made it highly sought after, even before his death in 1459, by the Dukes of Norfolk and Somerset as well as by the Duchess of York, the Earl of Warwick, Lord Scales, and Lord Beaumont.

STATUS AND PRIVACY

The exterior of a house was increasingly developed to make a statement about the status of the owner. It did so by its architectural form and scale, and by its decoration. The gatehouse came to be the most prominent feature of a frontage, sometimes heightened by its reflection in a broad moat, as at Herstmonceux Castle or Oxburgh Hall. Whereas the approach to Ightham Mote had been little more than an arched entry in 1332, it was converted into a three-storeyed tower by 1480. An imposing gatehouse underlined the hierarchical character of a house approach, being used by those of high rank, with staff often relegated to a subsidiary entry, as at Ightham Mote and Baddesley Clinton. Such gatehouses came to have many windows, as at Knole and Hadleigh Deanery, to distinguish them from their military predecessors and they were increasingly centred in a symmetrical composition to enhance their symbolic function, as at Thornbury Castle and Oxburgh Hall.

Coats of arms were a conspicuous display of local status, sometimes combined with those of a patron or leading neighbour. A panel above the entry at Lumley Castle (c.1390) holds the shields of Richard II and five northern families, while the tiered display on the gatehouse of Hylton Castle (c.1395) includes the arms of Richard II, the Bishop and Chancellor of Durham, and the friends of the builder, Sir William Hylton. An owner's arms were a prominent feature on the gatehouse of Thornbury Castle, between the front windows at Brympton d'Evercy, Somerset (1520s), and on the hall bay window at Bingham's Melcombe, Dorset (c.1555). The purses of the Lord Treasurer's office are conspicuously displayed above the inner entry of Lord Cromwell's Wingfield Manor, while the stone sheep holding the shield of Sir John Sydenham on the parapet of Brympton d'Evercy pointed to the source of his wealth.

The plan and appearance of a medieval house reflected the social structure of the family and household it was built to accommodate. At its heart was the hall, the domestic, social and administrative centre of any major household. Yet its function was not unchanging. During the twelfth and thirteenth centuries the hall was where meals were taken in common, domestic staff could sleep, tenants assembled, and justice was administered. It was cleared up and cleaned out every morning, for the hall was where the lord made his presence felt – physically, socially, and communally. But though its form and focal position barely changed throughout the fourteenth and fifteenth centuries there was a gradual modification in its use. As a result of the desire for greater privacy, a hall's function was increasingly limited to feasting, entertainment and formal receptions.

This cultural change was jump-started by Edward III through his redevelopment of the royal apartments at Windsor Castle. He demanded greater manpower resources for and incurred greater expenditure on his remodelling of this castle into a palace between 1353 and 1377 than on any other building project throughout his reign. Three sides of the upper court were reconstructed, with the principal range developed to provide a suitable setting for large-scale ceremonies and entertainment. His new hall and chapel, built back to back, were at first-floor level, no doubt reached by a now lost grand stair. The scale of this development and its lavish internal embellishment made a statement about Edward's political attitudes and military achievements during the first phase of the Hundred Years' War. His precept was quickly followed by John of Gaunt at Kenilworth Castle (1372–80), where part of the grand stair from the courtyard survives, as well as a dais window large enough to be a separate dining area with its own fireplace.

Leaving the hall to one side, the prime structural developments during the later Middle Ages occurred in the growth of private chambers and apartments, and in intriguingly different ways. It is worth underlining that while the changes were structural, the factors determining their development were inherently cultural. The status of an apartment depended on several factors. The most important was its relationship to the hall. If it was close to the offices and kitchen, it was usually of modest status. If it was beyond the high table at the upper end of the hall, then it was of high social status. Ground-floor rooms were of lower standing than those above, while the scale of the facilities, window size, and the presence of fireplaces and lavatories were indicative of the occupant's social position. A room's decorative qualities were also significant,

Kenilworth Castle, Warwickshire. John of Gaunt's first-floor hall, built of local sandstone, was well-windowed, enhanced by vertical panelling and heated by opposing fireplaces. Beyond that illustrated was a bay window opening off the dais. It was almost a small room and had its own hearth. Documents suggest that the dais was also warmed by triple fireplaces, no longer evident. The passage beyond marks the position of the corridor leading to Gaunt's private apartments.

including an elaborate roof structure in the case of upper rooms as well as architectural embellishment, painted glass, or painted decoration on the walls.

These factors translated into house development in a number of ways during the later Middle Ages. The most immediate and extended development was the substantial increase in chamber accommodation, and more specifically in the accommodation for the owner of a house and his family. The documentary evidence for royal houses, including Westminster, Clarendon and Woodstock, reveals the increase in the number of rooms needed by the king and queen under both Edward I and Edward II, even though there is barely any standing evidence today. But look at Ludlow, Bolton or Kenilworth castles and one can see how domestic accommodation expanded during the fourteenth century.

Externally, the Anglo-Norman castle at Ludlow is as impressive and as formidable as any built by Edward I in north Wales. Internally, as much care was taken with the layout of the residential accommodation in the years close to 1300 as previously with its military capacity (page 46). Furthermore, the accommodation of hall and associated chamber blocks and offices was carefully integrated with the defensive frontage so that its military function was in no way endangered. By the time that Lord Scrope built Bolton Castle between 1378 and 1396, the frowning exterior concealed a veritable warren of halls and chambers, skilfully interlocking, but ensuring privacy and scaled by size and facilities to the rank of the occupier (page 9). His contemporary John of Gaunt, Duke of Lancaster, did not see himself primarily as the leading magnate of England but as a prince on the European political stage. His peers were the rulers of Spain, the Low Countries and Brittany and the Valois princes of France rather than the Earls of Northumberland or Warwick. Nor did he see his patrimonial seat at Leicester as a fitting centre for his household; he chose instead to develop the already imposing, lake-protected and larger fortress at Kenilworth. His range of private apartments was a double sequence of two-storey chambers following the same plan at both levels, separated by a stair in the middle to give greater control and security to the innermost rooms, which terminated alongside a chapel. The whole ensemble, with its lavishly decorated façades, was built on a scale that matched the status of its owner and is as imposing today in its ruined state as it was awe-inspiring to Gaunt's contemporaries.

Chambers were not used for a single purpose, as most of ours are today, but were multi-functional. They might be a withdrawing chamber, a bedroom, a dressing and ablution room, or might equally be used for taking meals and receiving guests. The chambers were, however, usually of single social status. A lord's chamber was strictly out of bounds to all but him and those honoured few he cared to admit. Chambers increased not only in number but in the quality of their appointments. The number of lavatories and fireplaces at Ludlow, Windsor and Bolton castles shows that comfort was becoming increasingly important, and this began to apply to rooms used not only by the owner but by his guests and senior members of his household, who enjoyed a common lavatory tower at both Ludlow and Kenilworth castles. High-quality chambers were increasingly furnished with painted walls, tiled floors were laid, windows were decoratively

Mount Grace Priory, Yorkshire. Although this is the fifteenth-century cell of a Carthusian monk, the replica furniture gives an idea of a chamber's domestic appearance in c.1500. Its sparseness would have been offset by textiles and cushions in a secular context.

Bolton Castle. This chamber has lost most of its wall plaster but it would have been comfortable enough with a roaring fire and shuttered windows.

glazed, and tapestries were introduced from the close of the fourteenth century (see chapter 6). What is clear is that by concentrating on fewer residences than in the early Middle Ages it was possible for a major householder to expand the number of high-quality rooms in his house, and to furnish them appropriately with comfortable facilities and luxurious materials.

Raby Castle, County Durham. One of the largest palace-fortresses in medieval England, it was almost entirely developed as the power house of the Neville family during the twenty-one years between 1367 and 1388. The irregular scale and projection of the towers suggest enlargement in stages as against the regularised form of the slightly later residences at Bolton and Wressle.

Wressle Castle, Yorkshire. Only one range of this quadrangular palace-fortress survives, built of blocks of creamy ashlar. The balanced frontage conceals a complex internal plan, as is so often the case with mid to late fourteenth-century residences. The lord's tower (left) is separated from the chapel in the further tower by his personal rooms. As Sir Thomas Percy never married, Wressle was not built as a family home but as a residence reflecting his pedigree and distinguished state service.

The increase in the number of chambers and the growth of the household inevitably meant an increase in the size of a house. This, in turn, encouraged the development of the courtyard plan, bringing discipline to residential layouts. It has already been noted how the Neville family formalised the planning of their residences in north-east England during the later fourteenth century (pages 66–7). But it should also be noted that, while Brancepeth, Raby and Sheriff Hutton had long been important spheres of influence, they were now joined by the newly established centres of power at Wressle and Bolton initiated by Sir Thomas Percy (the younger son of the Earl of Northumberland) and Lord Scrope respectively.

Leconfield Manor (Yorkshire) no longer stands but it was not unlike Bolton and Wressle castles in its quadrangular and towered form with galleried lodging ranges for the yeomen (ground floor) and the gentlemen (first floor) attending the Earl of Northumberland, whose own apartments lay on the sunny south side of the house. But whereas most households could be accommodated round a single courtyard, those of the crown and some *nouveaux riches* came to need at least two courts, separated by the hall. This divided the staff accommodation, services, and stables from the more private rooms of the family. It also facilitated greater control over internal entry. First adopted towards the close of the fourteenth century, the form had become the norm for high-status houses by the second quarter of the fifteenth century as at Drayton House (Northamptonshire), Caister Castle, and Haddon Hall. The courtyard form also encouraged the development of a balanced façade. There was an attempt at this in the courtyard frontage of Edward III's residential development at Windsor Castle, but more satisfactory models can be seen at Bolton and Kenilworth castles. By then, the balanced façade had become an indication of superior status and sophisticated planning, exemplified during the fifteenth century at Herstmonceux and Bronsil castles, Great Chalfield Manor, and Shelton Hall, Norfolk (destroyed). It subsequently became a prime feature of early Tudor houses from Oxburgh Hall and Compton Wynyates to Hampton Court and Nonsuch Palace.

One further development during the fourteenth century was that of the lightly fortified house. One might assume that this meant a house with provision for defence from external attack, but the greater stability of the country by the mid fourteenth century made such provision unnecessary. However, that period was the great age of chivalry, and that icon of chivalry, Windsor Castle in its rebuilding under Edward III, was given two courtyard gatehouses with portcullises, battlements and loops, though they led to no more than a galleried courtyard in one instance and the kitchen area in the other. The initiative shown by the king's master mason was swiftly followed by others. The turrets, archery loops and gatehouse at Hever (c.1383) are less pretentious but have scant military capability. The drawbridge, portcullis, battlements and cannon openings at Kirby Muxloe (1480–4), a hundred years later, certainly give the residence a martial air that would have been of little use in practice. Some of the cannon openings were sited so that they would have hit an opposing tower.

Kirby Muxloe Castle, Leicestershire. In rebuilding his family home, Sir William Hastings worked within the framework of the earlier fortified house. The layout was old-fashioned, but the moated house was up-to-date in its pseudo-defensive arrangements and use of decorative brickwork.

Nor had Lord Hastings any enemies from whom he needed to protect himself: the opposite was true. These measures were externally impressive but were simply for show and splendour. They were the trappings of defence, not its reality. Their inclusion in fifteenth-century houses such as Oxburgh Hall, Faulkbourne Hall, Cotehele, and Tonford Manor (Kent) made a statement of lordship and status but was militarily irrelevant.

LODGINGS AND RESIDENTIAL TOWER-HOUSES

Courtyard development, balanced façades, increased privacy and the theatrical elements of defence could usually be accommodated within the framework of the earlier medieval house. But there were two new factors that could not be so accommodated and therefore warranted new house forms. One was the development of household lodgings. The second was the introduction of residential tower-houses. During the later Middle Ages, élite families developed larger and more elaborate households than previously and needed large-scale high-quality accommodation to house their members. This was usually served by two-storey ranges, with lower-grade staff living at ground level and superior staff at the upper level. Such units could be like dormitories, but they were more frequently divided into individual rooms. Each one, about 20 feet (6 metres) square, usually had its own entrance, window, fireplace and lavatory. It was the equivalent of a medieval bed-sitter. Lodgings on the upper floor might be reached by external stairs, as at Dartington Hall (c.1388–1400),

Dartington Hall, Devon. An engraving of the Hall made by the Buck brothers in 1734 shows that both sides of the outer court were fully lined with lodgings. They consisted of groups of four rooms at two levels, built to a high standard of comfort with separate entries, fireplaces and lavatories. The west range, shown here, with several projections marking the position of the outer stairs, was erected in c.1395–1400.

Above: *Haddon Hall, Derbyshire. Though built nearly a hundred years later than those at Dartington, this line of lodgings in the lower court is the finest preserved example in England with relatively unchanged interiors. The centre doorway opened on to the stair to the higher-quality upper rooms, with the flanking doorways serving only the ground-floor rooms. Such lodgings had become a corollary of seigniorial households from the mid fourteenth century to the late sixteenth.*

Left: *Haddon Hall. The imposing gateway and lodging tower, among the last additions to the Hall, were made by Sir Henry Vernon at the close of the fifteenth century after he had become a courtier of importance. The gateway, replacing the earlier one at the other end of this mansion, was not defensive but held six lodgings of different scale and quality. It should be compared with the guest tower at Wingfield Manor a generation earlier.*

or subsequently by balconied corridors as at Gainsborough Old Hall (1479–85). The origin of such lodgings can be found in early academic foundations at Oxford and Cambridge, but their application to large private houses first occurred in the 1340s. There are examples at Maxstoke Castle and Charing Palace of that date, followed by the vast ranges of lodgings lining two sides of the upper ward at Windsor Castle between about 1365 and 1377. Those at Dartington Hall are among the best-preserved in the country, lining two sides of the very large outer courtyard. They encompass forty-six individual and two communal lodgings. As each lodging was intended to be occupied by at least two men, those at Dartington were sufficient to house a complement of between 100 and 110 staff serving John Holand, Earl of Huntingdon, Richard II's half-brother.

The development of the discrete units that make up lodging ranges reflects the greater wealth and developing status and hierarchy of late medieval society. They continued to be built throughout the fifteenth century, as at Ewelme Manor, Oxfordshire (c.1420–50), Wingfield Manor and Haddon Hall, where the ranges include individual lodgings and two-roomed lodgings for superior members serving Sir Henry Vernon (died 1515), a leading Derbyshire knight. Early sixteenth-century lodgings are immediately identifiable at Thornbury Castle and Hampton Court Palace, and those of the mid century at Kirby Hall (Northamptonshire).

The second development, the residential tower-house, was a form equally limited to high-status houses. It was a development of the second quarter of the fifteenth century and continued to the end of that era. There is a common thread between Anglo-Norman keeps and the subsequent domestic version providing high-quality rooms in an imposing tower, such as that at Stokesay Castle (1284–96). Nor did the form entirely disappear during the fourteenth century. It occurs in the north of England at Edlingham, Belsay and spectacularly at Warkworth Castle, and in central and southern England during the second half of the century at Baginton (Warwickshire), Nunney (Somerset) and Wardour (Wiltshire) castles – though none of the latter were military fortresses but all grand houses with external defensive characteristics.

Henry V was responsible for the regeneration of the tower-house as an

Stokesay Castle, Shropshire. The south tower of c.1290 was a lavish addition to the slightly earlier family block of this fortified house. Providing spacious self-contained accommodation on three floors, it more than doubled the owner's private rooms as well as creating a focal point for his residence.

Tattershall Castle, Lincolnshire. This imposing brick-built tower-house stands in almost complete condition, except for the small lead-covered spires that capped the corner turrets until the nineteenth century. The defensive-looking machicolated roof galleries are at variance with the large windows in each face.

important residential structure when he initiated a massive stone-towered complex at Sheen (now Richmond) in Surrey in 1414 and enclosed it with a 25 feet (7.6 metres) wide moat separating it from the remainder of his residence and his courtiers. Nothing survives of this palace, but it may have been influenced by the precepts of the French royal palaces at the Louvre and Vincennes, which had been residentially enhanced by Charles V between 1364 and 1380.

The royal precedent was immediately adopted by the nobility, led by Ralph, Lord Cromwell. His tower-house at Tattershall Castle is first mentioned in 1445 but it may have been commenced earlier as part of the building work initiated in 1434. This 110 feet (34 metres) high five-storey structure is a brick-built power house. The plan is of one large room at each level, with the comfort of fireplaces, garderobes, corner closets, decorated passages and hooks for tapestries. This tower is positioned next to the great hall and provided retiring rooms for the family, with

each floor offering greater privacy than that below, culminating in the top floor used by Cromwell and his wife as their privy bed-chamber.

Cromwell built a second residential tower-house at Wingfield Manor in the years immediately before 1450. Again five-storey with comfortably furnished chambers, this tower has – in addition to individual lavatories on each floor – two ground-floor communal

South Kyme Tower, Lincolnshire. This four-storey tower is a major precursor of that at Tattershall 8 miles away. Built in the mid fourteenth century as a residential tower to the lost hall of the Umfraville family, it was inherited and occupied in 1437 by Lord Cromwell's great friend and companion, Walter Tailboy. The Tattershall tower-house is first mentioned in the building accounts for that castle a year after Tailboy's death in 1444.

Above left: *Wingfield Manor. The High Tower was built in the south-west angle of the inner court and still commands the whole site. It was one of the later phases of Lord Cromwell's development of this palace-mansion before his death here in 1456.*

Above right: *Wingfield Manor. Only two sides survived the partial destruction of the High Tower in 1646. Nevertheless, the plan of its five storeys is clear – a comfortable and well-lit heated room on each floor with an adjacent lavatory.*

lavatories for staff, cleaned by rain water channelled from the roof. The Tattershall and Wingfield towers each hold a self-contained sequence of elegant rooms in vertical mode but, whereas Tattershall was next to the great hall and used by Cromwell and his family, the tower at Wingfield is nowhere near the great hall but adjacent to two lodging ranges. It was probably used for high-ranking officials or favoured guests. The entertainment of guests was an important element in a medieval household; it was considered a mark of munificence and generosity. Some analyses of household accounts show that visitors – from magnates to workmen – in some bishops' households accounted for between 20 and 30 per cent of those present at meal times, while the figure for the Duke of Buckingham's household at Thornbury Castle was between 44 and 50 per cent. The late fourteenth-century poem *Sir Gawain and the Green Knight* records the courteous reception and high-quality accommodation accorded an honoured guest – the tower at Wingfield Manor may well have been just the sort of accommodation that he would have enjoyed.

The purpose of these dominating residential tower-houses is usually clear from their position within the layout of a residence. Those sited beyond the upper end of the hall, as at Tattershall Castle, or at the upper end of a range of private apartments, as at Gainsborough Old Hall, served as the personal apartments for the family. Those positioned further away from the family area, as at Wingfield Manor or Minster Lovell Hall, Oxfordshire (*c*.1460), would have been used primarily for important guests or possibly leading household officials. Contemporary documents are not specific and there was probably no hard and fast rule, so such functions should not be pushed too far to exclude others. What is not in doubt is that such towers were residential in purpose, handsome in design, of high occupational status, and often with embellished decoration.

There are about thirty such structures spanning the years to the close of the fifteenth century. A number were raised in the later years of Henry VI's reign, including one possibly for Queen Margaret at Tutbury Castle (*c*.1457) and one

Sudeley Castle, Gloucestershire. The so-called Dungeon Tower is the largest one at this trophy mansion of Sir Ralph Boteler. The single apartment at each level was approached by a stair from the south range, now grass-covered but possibly the site of the great hall. A comparable group of high-quality rooms at the lower end of the hall had just been erected by Boteler's friend at Wingfield Manor.

Buckden Palace, Cambridgeshire. The tower-house of the Bishops of Lincoln with rooms on three floors above a half basement. Instead of the usual single apartment on each floor, the windows in this tower identify a more complex plan of rooms at each level. The foundations of a similar brick-built episcopal tower-house were found at Esher Palace, Surrey, in 2005.

by Sir Ralph Boteler (Treasurer of England in succession to Lord Cromwell) at Sudeley Castle (1441–58). Even more were built in Edward IV's reign, including the Closet Tower at Raglan Castle by the Earl of Pembroke (*c.*1465), those at Esher Palace (Surrey, 1462–72) and Farnham Castle (1470–5), for Bishop Waynflete, and at Buckden Palace for Bishop Rotherham (1472–80), and the great brick tower at Faulkbourne Hall built by Sir Thomas Montgomery, one of Edward IV's trusted advisers, in the years after 1465. The advent of a Tudor monarch made no difference to the preferred forms and style of the previous generation. The thirteenth Earl of Oxford built massive brick tower-houses at Hedingham Castle, Essex (1485–98), and at Castle Camps, Cambridgeshire (late fifteenth century), both since pulled down. The last residential tower-house was raised by Henry VII at Greenwich in 1499, its foundations exposed in 1970.

Residential tower-houses were a conspicuous statement by an élite society over a seventy-year period. They were versatile as good-quality accommodation for family, guests and leading officials, capable of being built in stone or brick, and were limited to central and southern England. They were not, however, solely an English phenomenon but occur in Flanders, France and Spain. But they were quickly discarded early in the sixteenth century when the need for greater privacy was answered with a more fashionable form. This change in planning design swiftly led to the overriding triumph of the double-courtyard plan with separate apartments for the king and queen or the magnate and his wife in an aristocratic residence. Apartments were now built in horizontal rather than vertical mode, fused in ranges round the inner court in a sequence of increasingly private rooms or suites. This was the form adopted by the Duke of Buckingham at Thornbury Castle (1510–21), by Cardinal Wolsey at Hampton Court (1516–26) and by Henry VIII in several of his regal palaces.

Dartington Hall. The hall, lower residential block and kitchen of John Holand's Devon mansion from the site of the inner court.

TROPHY HOUSES

The house built at Dartington at the close of the fourteenth century not only displays a double-courtyard plan with some of the private apartments of Richard II's half-brother probably extending to the inner court, but also two lodging ranges lining the outer court to accommodate the hierarchical society of his household. Equally significant is that Dartington Hall is the earliest prime residence of the nobility that is entirely domestic in character. Unlike almost every other house built by John Holand's fellow magnates during the later fourteenth century, all the appurtenances of defence, genuine or otherwise – drawbridge, portcullis, towers, wall-walks and machicolations – are totally absent. Dartington Hall was not even moated.

This is the first of a new type of residence, a prestigious reflection of its owner's ennoblement, a public statement of his standing and – in this case – his royal relationship, marked by the badges of Richard II and John Holand on the central boss of the hall porch vault. Intended to be the dynastic centre of the younger branch of this now semi-royal family, Dartington Hall was palace-like in scale but totally domestic in appearance. This Devon mansion was the first of a sequence of fifteenth-century houses known as trophy houses. They were characterised by five factors. First, they were built on new sites, or on earlier sites stripped of all previous buildings. Second, they were entirely residential in character. This is the point when the castle was finally domesticated, although a few superficial trappings of military character might survive to give the place greater status. Third, they were developed round two or more courtyards to provide adequate household lodgings, as well as a sequence of family and guest accommodation. Fourth, they were usually completed during the owner's lifetime. Finally, they reflected the owner's achievements, either as an officer of state, on the battlefield or through his recent ennoblement from the gentry class.

The greater houses of the fifteenth century were not built by the crown or the leading members of the aristocracy, lay or ecclesiastical. They made some modest additions to their properties, like the hall added by Edward IV at Eltham

136

Palace (c.1475–80), or the tower-house by Bishop Rotherham at Buckden Palace, but no major residential projects were undertaken by such long-established families as the Percys, the Nevilles, the Mortimers, the Fitzalans or the Beauchamps. They continued to live in the castles and palace-fortresses built by earlier generations. The leading houses of the fifteenth century were erected by *arriviste* knights or minor magnates, often built to a scale as large as, and sometimes surpassing, those of long-established families. In most cases, they are exemplars of the *nouveau riche* of the later Middle Ages and virtually all were developed in central and southern England.

John Holand, who had built Dartington Hall, lost his head in the aftermath of Richard II's deposition, and that event also cut short the building boom that had characterised Richard's reign. The uncertainties of Henry IV's rule and the reopening of the war with France under Henry V meant that most people's priorities lay elsewhere. But major building projects were rekindled during the 1430s by returning veterans, who used their spoils of war to initiate a sequence of trophy houses. Sir John Fastolf's achievements in northern France were proclaimed in East Anglia by the construction of his fortified house at Caister (1432–45), just as Baron Lovel's service in the wars up to 1431 was followed by the development of Minster Lovell Hall in Oxfordshire (1431–40). Hampton Court, Sir Rowland Lenthall's house on the Welsh border near Leominster, reflected the rewards of court service as well as the profits of war (c.1434–47). But the most imposing one of them all from this period was Wingfield Manor, proudly identifying Lord Cromwell's ten-year tenure as an effective Treasurer of England. Wingfield was more formal in layout than Dartington Hall and more obviously domestic than Caister Castle, but the scale and development of Cromwell's personal accommodation, the sequence of lodging ranges to meet

Dartington Hall, Devon. This semi-royal hall of c.1390 is on the grandest scale. Note the early example of a dais fireplace. The apartment was re-roofed by William Weir in the early 1930s following the form but not the precise character of the original hammer-beam roof.

137

Minster Lovell Hall, Oxfordshire. The much ruined house of William, Lord Lovel, was built round three sides of a courtyard, with the fourth side still open to the river Windrush. The hall, shown here, was approached from the cross-passage (right). It had particularly high windows to allow for wall-hangings below.

the social standing of the occupants, and the massive lodging tower mark out Wingfield Manor as a trophy house of enormous scale and panache.

The equally spectacular contemporary residence of Sir Roger Fiennes at Herstmonceux (*c*.1438–49) might look architecturally defensible, particularly the gatehouse, but the towers are not strong, and its capacity to withstand serious assault was feeble. What Fiennes was subtly suggesting was a statement of lordship and of a rank rather greater than knighthood implied. Internally, the planning had become more complex than that of Wingfield, with two-storey

Hampton Court, Herefordshire. The gatehouse and chapel (left) are original structures of Sir Rowland Lenthall's imposing house, crenellated under licence in 1434. The flanking ranges have been much altered, not least between 1835 and 1845, when the house became a 122-room mansion.

Sudeley Castle. Before ascending the throne, Richard, Duke of Gloucester, held Sudeley Castle from 1469 to 1478 as his power-base before the growth of his northern 'empire'. He was responsible for redeveloping a suite of three well-lit ground-floor rooms, with movement from left to right, which gave access for favoured visitors via the newel (behind the tree) to the magnificent first-floor presence chamber. The skeletal framework of its outer wall reveals a ripped-out fireplace, flanked by floor-to-roof windows, one of them a bay (left).

ranges of apartments grouped round four rather than one or two courtyards (three of them were cloistered with first-floor galleries to facilitate communication). Fashionably built in brick, Herstmonceux's paramount domestic character and deliberately landscaped moat identify it as a particularly spirited trophy house by a leading gentleman of the royal household and its treasurer between 1439 and 1446.

Sir Ralph Boteler succeeded Cromwell as Treasurer of England in 1443 and was subsequently steward of the royal household for ten years. Boteler's residence at Sudeley (1441–58) had the double-courtyard plan, lodging ranges and residential tower of the trophy house even before its subsequent enhancement within twenty years by Richard, Duke of Gloucester. The list could be extended during the second half of the fifteenth century by such houses as Stourton House in Wiltshire (c.1450), Gainsborough Old Hall (1462–80), Treago Castle (1460s) and Kirby Muxloe Castle (1480–4), and such trophy houses were still being built during the early years of Henry VII's rule, as at Hedingham Castle and the Earl of Derby's mansion at Lathom in Lancashire (c.1485–95). However, Henry soon showed himself to be reluctant to create new peers, and their number fell to forty-two in 1509. The king's officials were now rewarded by no more than knighthoods, and few were in a position to undertake the building of a new trophy house.

However, Edward Stafford, third Duke of Buckingham, bucked the trend. Like Lord Cromwell of Wingfield and Tattershall, he enjoyed greater prestige and status than his forebears and built accordingly. He laid the foundation stone of his new residence at Thornbury in Gloucestershire in October 1511. It was a

Thornbury Castle, Gloucestershire. The family apartments of the third Duke of Buckingham faced the privy garden, still enclosed by its contemporary galleried wall-walk. The three full-height bay windows to differing plans are made more voluptuous at the upper level for they lit the Duke's apartments, whereas those of his wife were at ground level.

magnificent double-courtyard house with an outer court of household lodgings and suites of apartments for the Duke and his wife on two separate floors filling one side of the inner court. They were built horizontally rather than vertically, overlooking a private garden in a sequence of increasing privacy. But the mansion was also seen as a potential power base that might threaten the stability and established order of Henry VIII's kingdom. Thornbury Castle was not only a glorious palace-mansion, but with its builder's summary execution at the King's orders in 1521, it became the swan-song of the late medieval trophy house in England.

10. Comparative residences

Large houses served a community of people – the lord, his household, staff and retainers. But there were a considerable number of other buildings serving residential communities during the Middle Ages and with a similar approach to layout, functional planning and design standards. Some were religious foundations such as granges, colleges of priests and the houses of monastic heads, while others were of an educational purpose, including the schools for young students at Winchester and Eton, and the colleges for more mature students at Oxford and Cambridge. Though of differing purpose, their buildings were designed for the similar function and common culture of living, dining and enclosure protection. Their structural development impinged on and influenced those of larger houses so that a consideration of buildings serving a religious, scholastic, or quasi-military community can illuminate the form of those in a lay environment.

MONASTIC FOUNDATIONS

There were more than eight hundred religious houses in England and over fifty in Wales at the time of their dissolution during the late 1530s, providing permanent residence to communities of monks, nuns and lay brethren. As with domestic houses, they varied in size but provided a support system not unlike that found in lay households. Most of the stone buildings erected during the twelfth and early thirteenth centuries lasted throughout a community's

Haughmond Abbey, Shropshire. The abbot's dining hall is the dominant feature of this site, wholly secular in layout and purpose. Built in c.1350, this hall is larger than that at Stokesay Castle not far away. As there was no need for a chamber above the services in this Augustinian community, the larger west window, with evidence of its multi-traceried head, would have given the hall a more ecclesiastical character than its secular counterpart.

existence, though there were some notable late rebuildings, including the abbey churches at Wigmore (Herefordshire) and Sherborne (Dorset), and the cloisters at Gloucester and Lacock (Wiltshire). But the trend towards increased privacy and comfort in lay households during the later Middle Ages was also mirrored in monastic communities. Dormitories were partitioned to provide separate sleeping cubicles and guest quarters were built to higher standards than previously, while the head of the community was given generous and sometimes lavish accommodation that in many cases resulted in its sequestration and similar lay use after Henry VIII ordered the dissolution of all monasteries.

Architecturally, *refectories* were similar to secular halls but used for dining purposes by ecclesiastics instead of laymen. They were usually on a large scale, as superior in display as their secular counterparts, with a dais at the end furthest from the entrance for the head of the community, senior officers and important visitors, and long tables with benches along the side walls of the hall for the rest of the community. The only differentiating element was a pulpitum towards the dais end for readings from the Bible and theological works during meals. Examples include the Norman survival at Horsham St Faith (Norfolk), with its brilliant late thirteenth- and early fourteenth-century wall-paintings; that at Beaulieu (Hampshire, *c.*1230), converted after the Dissolution into the parish church; and Denny Priory (Cambridgeshire, *c.*1350), where the contemporary platform for the tables and benches and tiled floor have been revealed. Monastic *kitchens* were no different structurally from those for large households, as the surviving examples at Glastonbury (Somerset, *c.*1340) and Durham Priory (*c.*1370) illustrate when compared with those at Raby Castle (*c.*1380), and Dartington Hall (*c.*1390).

Dormitories were always at first-floor level, with the beds lining both sides of the room, allowing no privacy. Few dormitories have survived for they seem to have been singled out for destruction by Henry VIII's commissioners to deter reoccupation, but there are high-quality roofed survivals at Cleeve Abbey (mid thirteenth century), Valle Crucis Abbey (Denbighshire, late fourteenth century), and Durham Priory (1398–1405), which retain the partition slots for individual cubicles. They are a valuable parallel to the ruined dormitories at Wingfield Manor and Cawood Castle.

The *lodging* for the head of a monastic community is of particular relevance to domestic architecture. As it was the residence for a person of rank, often of considerable social and political standing in larger foundations, abbots' and priors' houses frequently became miniature versions of a small manor house, with the hall separating the service end from the withdrawing chamber, chapel and bedchamber of the monastic head. They were equally a place for the entertainment of important guests, but towards the close of the Middle Ages, comfort, status and rank (so far as the outside world was concerned) became increasingly paramount and were reflected in the development and opulence of the accommodation.

Most of the monastic houses that survive are in their late stage of development but they are sufficiently numerous and of such high calibre to warrant separate study in their own right. They are sometimes ruined, as at Rievaulx, Monk Bretton and Kirkstall (a particularly large and early example of *c.*1230), all in Yorkshire, partially roofed at Castle Acre (Norfolk), complete but empty at Cleeve and Valle Crucis, or still inhabited at Battle (Sussex), Forde

(Dorset), Watton (Yorkshire) and Wenlock (Shropshire). Abbots' and priors' lodgings were particularly susceptible to secular occupation after their dissolution between 1536 and 1540. They were ready-made homes and could even be enlarged by incorporating parts of a nearby claustral range, as at Watton Priory and at Newstead Abbey (Nottinghamshire). The two-storey lodging at Wenlock Priory, one of the most complete and well-preserved medieval houses in England, has a single sweeping stone roof covering the sequence of rooms and the multi-windowed ambulatory that accessed them. Built in *c*.1430, this residence was initially divided into two – one end for the infirmarer, whose hall was adjacent, with the remainder occupied by the prior – but the two parts are now united in a single residence with retained original interiors and fittings, paved floors and octagonal stone tables in the windows of the prior's hall and withdrawing chamber. The abbot's hall at Forde, with its highly impressive entry porch, has been little touched since its construction in *c*.1528, while the abbot's parlour of *c*.1470 at Muchelney retains its splendid fireplace with decorated lintel, space above for a lost wall-painting surmounted by carved stone lions, and a panelled bench of *c*.1500 nearby (page 89).

By this time such lodgings had become a background to equally striking furnishings, emphasising the cult of magnificence and display. If bishops and archbishops lived like barons, leading abbots and priors were not going to be outdone. In addition to the extensive accommodation, splendid ceilings, and chapel wall-paintings of *c*.1470 in the prior's house at Durham (now the Deanery), documentary evidence shows that the bedrooms were hung with prized red fabrics under Prior Wessington (1424–36), the chapel was furnished with luxurious vestments and jewellery, while the buttery held a valuable

Muchelney Abbey, Somerset. The residential range of this Benedictine abbey is made up of the fourteenth-century kitchen block (left), the imposing frontage of the late fifteenth-century abbot's lodging, and the ruined dining hall of c.1500. The roofed kitchen and lodging have survived through continuous farmhouse use between 1540 and 1927.

Durham: the Deanery. The house of the priors of Durham reflects its on-going occupation since the thirteenth century. Now the house of the dean of the cathedral, it was on a scale comparable with many secular residences. The principal apartments are on the first floor, with the prior's chamber (left) and projecting chapel lined with wall-paintings (right).

collection of silver rather than pewter or tin. The rebuilding and decorative lavishness of many late medieval monastic lodgings was not symptomatic of monastic decay as promulgated by Henry VIII's commissioners but a response, like that of many wealthy laymen, to the fashion for thoroughgoing domestic rehabilitation. It was a reflection of their prosperity and of the need to meet a convent's responsibility for hospitality to secular visitors of all ranks. This extended from magnates, knights and local gentlemen to fellow dignitaries, monastic officials and monks from other houses. This factor of hospitality was not only a way of life, as active as in any secular household, but it was seen as an obligation, though one that could become an expensive liability, particularly when the king or a leading magnate with his retinue descended on a community as King James I of Scotland did on Durham Priory in 1424, followed by Cardinal Beaufort (1429), the future Pope Pius II (1436) and Henry VI (1448).

As well as the accommodation for monastic heads, there is documentary evidence that some other senior officials had their own lodgings at an early date. Though the structural evidence for this is rare, the house built by the sacrist Alan of Walsingham for himself near the infirmary at Ely in 1333–6 still stands relatively complete (as does the prior's house with its chapel, a gem of fourteenth-century England). The practice subsequently developed of allowing lay people to be given accommodation, food and drink in return for a substantial advance payment. The two self-contained lodgings below the

144

Cleeve Abbey, Somerset. This Cistercian foundation prospered during the mid fifteenth century under Abbot Juyner, who rebuilt this range. The broad arch spanned the washing basin next to the entrance and steps to the first-floor refectory. Flooded with light from both sides, this dining hall is one of the most sumptuous in southern England. Below it were a pair of spacious lodgings, probably for corrodians.

abbot's hall at Cleeve may have been for such people, known as corrodians or pensioners. Another example of the provision of individual rooms was the practice of the austere Carthusian order for each monk to occupy a lodging in which he ate, slept, worked and meditated in almost total seclusion. One such two-storeyed lodging at Mount Grace Priory in Yorkshire has been fully restored and furnished (page 125).

Monastic *precincts* are comparable to the outer court of a secular residence for they served a similar purpose with their enclosing wall, gateway, guest accommodation, bakehouse, brewhouse and offices. In many cases these monastic yards can give us a better idea of an outer court than secular survivals for, in contrast with the latter, many such monastic sites have never been built over after their destruction and abandonment. The thirteenth-century guest house at Kirkstall Abbey has been excavated and left exposed, that of Ely Priory (*c.*1330) is now occupied by the bishop and school, while Lacock retains its brewhouse of *c.*1540. Few of the many gatehouses that survive were built for defensive reasons, except for those at Bury St Edmunds (Suffolk), Thornton (Lincolnshire), and Ewenni (Glamorgan). Apart from controlling access, they were used for support functions – dispensing alms, a courtroom, guest lodgings – as in private houses with smaller gateways, like that at Wetheral Priory (Cumbria, fifteenth century), indistinguishable from a secular one such as that at Steeton Hall.

Whereas the income for some orders such as the Augustinians came mainly from impropriated churches, the Cistercians and Premonstratensians made considerable use of farmed land. This necessitated the establishment of *granges* on their larger holdings, in essence farms staffed by lay brothers until the Black Death and its aftermath encouraged the practice of leasing to outsiders. Bordesley Abbey, Worcestershire, for instance, had twenty granges by the early thirteenth century within a 23 mile radius of the precinct, though none of the medieval buildings survived beyond the mid nineteenth century. Nor did these farms conform to any regular plan but they differed little from a small manor house except in the greater prominence given to barns and other farm buildings. Often used by the head of a community and his monks as a rural retreat, the grange at Salmestone, Kent (St Augustine's, Canterbury) stands almost complete, while those at Iford, Sussex (Lewes Priory), Tisbury, Wiltshire (Shaftesbury Abbey), and Forthampton, Gloucestershire (Tewkesbury Abbey), are altered but still inhabited. The barn of *c.*1300 at Great Coxwell (Beaulieu Abbey) is like a vast windowless aisled hall while the slightly later grange barns at Leigh, Worcestershire (Pershore Abbey), and Bradford on Avon, Wiltshire (Shaftesbury Abbey), are equally spectacular with their cleared floor space.

ECCLESIASTICAL FOUNDATIONS

More than half the cathedrals of England were monastic (e.g. Canterbury, Gloucester) with the remainder in the hands of secular clergy (e.g. Wells, Salisbury). The latter were run by canons who gradually appointed junior

Wells, Somerset: Vicars' Close. This street of priests' houses, with its prominent line of chimneys, reflects continuous occupation since its development in 1348. Each house consisted of a large ground-floor living room (with a lavatory under the stair) leading to a similarly sized bedchamber above. Both rooms had fireplaces. There were originally forty-two houses but some have been joined together and their windows enlarged, particularly during the eighteenth century. The walled front gardens were an early fifteenth-century addition.

Chichester, Sussex: Vicars' Close. Built between 1394 and 1404, the two lines of twelve houses terminate in the contemporary dining hall. These twenty-four houses followed the same plan as those at Wells but the vicars declined in number and were allowed to marry, bringing alterations and extensions over the centuries until the institution's dissolution in 1935.

priests or *vicars choral* to carry out the liturgical functions in their place between the fourteenth and early sixteenth centuries. To ensure moral and organisational discipline, all such vicars were subject to a quasi-monastic discipline in colleges within the cathedral close. Nine are known to have existed, with important survivals at Lincoln (1270–1310), Wells (*c.*1348) and Chichester (*c.*1396), where they dined in common, retired to a common parlour and slept in individual chambers. A precursor of the educational colleges at Oxford and Cambridge, vicars choral exemplify how a modest professional group expressed their rapid rise in status through their architecture.

From the mid fourteenth century a new type of foundation developed under private and episcopal patronage centred on a *chantry*, where intercessory masses were recited for the health or soul of the founder. The endowments for these masses took the form of lands, rents, tenements and money and were given by people of all ranks to churches across the country. To bring discipline to the very considerable number of priests who responded to the pious needs of such benefactors, the more wealthy patrons would build a house close to the parish church, while the wealthiest would fund a college for communal living. Such colleges were not laid out to a pre-ordained plan but included the same structural elements as in colleges of vicars choral. Smaller foundations such as Carnary College, Norwich, would be built as a single range while larger establishments were grouped round a small quadrangle, as at Cobham (1362), Maidstone (1395) and Wye (1432), all in Kent. There would be an entry gate, as at Maidstone and Manchester, where the college of 1421–45 is an outstanding and particularly complete survival of late medieval domestic architecture. All these colleges were suppressed under the Chantries Act of 1547 except for the royal college of St George within the precincts of Windsor Castle, which still fulfills an ecclesiastical residential function. Manchester is a musical academy, Cobham is an almshouse, Maidstone serves an educational purpose, and Wye is the heart of an agricultural college.

The estates of the *Knights Templars* and *Knights Hospitallers* were never numerous in England but each order held about seventy. After the suppression of the Templars in 1308, the Hospitallers received most of their lands. Both military orders combined working farms with an element of monastic austerity. A particularly clearly laid-out Templar property was that at South Witham in Lincolnshire, excavated during the 1960s because it had not been occupied since its abandonment in 1311. Like many monastic granges, the twelfth-century courtyard complex included three thatched barns, a metal workshop and a residential unit of hall, solar, chapel and separate kitchen with five ovens. A detached storeyed building may have been a first-floor dormitory for farm workers while nearby were a mill and several fishponds. The Templars' pre-1220 aisled hall survives at Temple Balsall, Warwickshire, as does their thirteenth-century chamber block at Strood, but these two orders followed no standard form for the layout of their properties.

The houses of *parish priests* have often disappeared while the church they served has survived. The reasons vary but the modern practice of the Church Commissioners of selling all Georgian and Victorian vicarages to lighten their financial burden has long-established precedents. It is surprising that so many such houses have survived (usually in private hands today), but they fall within

Stoke sub Hamdon Priory, Somerset. Not a priory but a house built for the five priests serving the chantry founded by Lord Beauchamp in 1304, and to serve as the centre of the farm that was their endowment and source of income. The house was rebuilt in 1444 with the porch opening into the hall (right), a first-floor chapel (left) and the priests' rooms to the rear. The forecourt is still filled with thatched stables, a cattle shed, two barns, a cart shed and a dovecote.

148

Hadleigh Deanery, Suffolk. This imposing gate-tower on the edge of the churchyard at Hadleigh is the only surviving part of a major residence planned by Archdeacon Pykenham. Built in c.1495, it is a display of wealth and patronage on a scale and with decoration that vies with contemporary structures at Buckden Palace, Faulkbourne Hall and, particularly, Sir Edmund Bedingfield's mansion at Oxburgh.

the main stream of domestic planning, varying from the modest to the impressive, depending on the scale of the endowment and the patronage of the local medieval landowner. Buckland Rectory in Gloucestershire is indistinguishable from a small manor house with its hall of c.1470 with central hammer-beam truss and painted window glass, flanked by the two-storeyed offices and solar blocks at opposing ends on a scale suitable for entertaining guests. Not surprisingly, priests' houses reflect the character of their locality. The rectory at Hadleigh is an impressive brick gatehouse of

Farleigh Hungerford Castle, Somerset: priests' house. This single house was erected in 1430 next to the chapel within the castle for the two priests serving the chantry founded by Sir Walter Hungerford in memory of his father. The priests lived here until the dissolution of all chantries in 1540, when it became a private house, doubled in length (left) during the seventeenth century.

*c.*1490, built by William Pykenham, Archdeacon of Suffolk, while some of the houses in Northumbria are of a defensive character, like those at Corbridge and Elsdon. The late fourteenth-century priest's house at Muchelney in Somerset is a smaller version of the gentry house of *c.*1420 at nearby Croscombe, while those in the south-east at Alfriston (Sussex) and Otham (Kent) are indistinguishable from other Wealden houses in the region. Some houses, particularly in the south-west, were for two or more priests serving rural parishes. Stone-built and dating from the fifteenth century, they were on a larger scale and, through long-standing ecclesiastical ownership, stand in fine condition at Trent (Dorset), Sampford Peverell (Devon), Congresbury (Somerset) and Farleigh Hungerford, but these are houses of the more wealthy benefices, whereas those of Chaucer's 'poor parson' have been lost.

EDUCATIONAL FOUNDATIONS

Of all the buildings analogous to larger secular houses during the later Middle Ages, William Wykeham's collegiate foundations at Winchester and Oxford were as revolutionary in concept as they were spectacular in execution. Their educational significance lies outside the scope of this book, but their architectural importance was equally dynamic. As Bishop of Winchester (1367–1404), Wykeham was determined to raise the educational standards of the clergy by establishing a school for ninety-nine boys at Winchester that would be preparatory to their advanced curriculum at New College, Oxford. This conjunction of junior and senior foundations on a majestic scale was unprecedented in Europe, as were the size and quality of his buildings. New

Oxford: New College. William Wykeham's foundation was mainly constructed between 1380 and 1387 and has not been radically altered since then. The entry overlooks the approach and the quadrangle, with the chapel (right) and some of the lodgings (left).

150

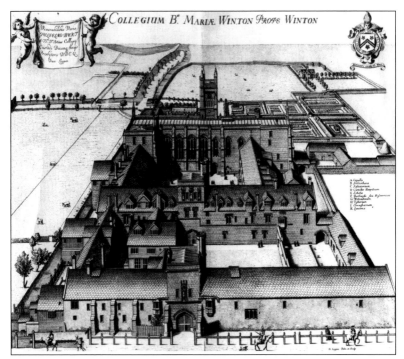

Winchester College, Hampshire: engraving by David Loggan, 1675. This bird's eye view illustrates a residence that has little changed since its construction between 1387 and 1401. It is a pathfinder in the development of schools in England and Wales but also plays a significant role in late medieval house development. It is centred on the same facilities of hall, kitchen, services and lodgings, organised in this instance round two formally planned courtyards. Apart from its imposing scale, the college also enjoyed two commanding gateways, a spacious layout, and high building standards.

College was erected between 1380 and 1386, followed by Winchester College between 1387 and 1401. Both foundations are key buildings of their period through their lordly scale in the newly developed Perpendicular style, but Winchester is particularly significant because of its spacious layout, logical design, and high standards. Just as Edward III's redevelopment of the residential apartments at Windsor was the primary building project of the third quarter of the fourteenth century, with major ramifications for domestic architecture (and overseen by Wykeham as Surveyor of the King's Works between 1356 and 1361), so it was also father to two magnificent sons, who in turn created a broader progeny. Furthermore most of Wykeham's buildings survive, not radically altered, and still used for their original purpose.

At both establishments, the principal units of hall, kitchen and offices, chapel and residential accommodation were logically and formally grouped round a quadrangle approached through a towered gateway, which gave the building presence as well as an eyrie for the all-seeing warden. As at Windsor, hall and chapel were built back to back to fill one side of the quadrangle with the accommodation filling two further sides, closed by the gateway on the fourth.

Oxford: Magdalen College. Like Wykeham, Bishop Waynflete was not only Bishop of Winchester and Chancellor of England (1456) but he also founded a college at Oxford. Magdalen rivalled New College in scale, organisation and architectural realisation. The college gateway is grander than Wykeham's, and a splendid example of the architectural exuberance of Edward IV's reign.

Whereas these units and the library had previously existed independently at Oxford, what was totally new was that all the functions were brought together in a coherent plan with the less prestigious buildings (kitchen, offices, cloister) built out of immediate sight. What was equally radical was providing accommodation for junior and senior members in the same range, with the younger members at Oxford in lodgings rather than the dormitories favoured at Winchester.

Begun seven years after New College, the Winchester foundation benefited from some of the problems encountered at Oxford through its development on a constricted site within a walled town. The main court at Winchester was set back upon an open area outside the city walls, allowing an outer court to contain all the services – stables, brewhouse, granary and slaughterhouse – so that the inner court could be entirely residential. In adopting this double-courtyard plan, the master mason and overseer, William Wynford, consolidated a domestic layout that had hitherto been only partly realised in contemporary buildings such as Dartington Hall or limited by earlier structures, as at New College and Windsor Castle. Furthermore, this twin-courtyard plan became a further refinement for houses of a multi-layered society under a secular head. It also encouraged an imposing gateway (one to each court at Winchester), contributing to the drama of approach that was repeated to a greater or lesser extent in all succeeding colleges as well as in such fifteenth-century mansions as Knole, Wingfield Manor, Herstmonceux and Oxburgh Hall.

Both educational foundations adopted the first-floor hall, a feature chosen by the previous generation for buildings of the highest status, as at Windsor and Kenilworth castles, but Wykeham confirmed its suitability for communal foundations of standing as much as for more domestic environments. The two-storeyed form of individual heated lodgings, severally occupied, had not been seen before on such a scale outside Windsor and was immediately adopted at Dartington Hall, followed by those at Ewelme Manor, Wingfield Manor and Winchester's Hospital of St Cross. The towers built for the muniments and valuables at both colleges were also followed in a modified form at some

Oxford: Magdalen College. The windows of the hall, like those at New College, were smaller than those of the more important chapel next to it. The oriel lighting the dais was an innovative feature in Oxford. The panelling is early sixteenth-century, while the roof is a copy of 1902 derived from the smoke silhouettes in the end walls.

leading residences (Bolton Castle, Minster Lovell Hall, Ashby de la Zouch Castle), while the facilities of both warden's lodgings were miniature versions of those found in a major household.

As befitted clerical establishments, both foundations were essentially inward-facing, with few windows to the outside world, but as much care was given to their design quality and variety as if these foundations had been an episcopal palace. The glass was among the best of its time, the chapel roofs were of innovative design, the statues were well carved, the window tracery was relatively austere, while the powerful linear style did not preclude rich mouldings. Wykeham's concept was the precedent for Henry VI's twin educational foundations at Eton and King's College, Cambridge, in the mid fifteenth century, as it was a generation later for those of Bishop Waynflete of Winchester at Magdalen School and College, Oxford. New College was the architectural prototype followed by all colleges at Oxford and Cambridge for the next two hundred years, but, even more than the Oxford establishment, Winchester College was the template for the equally structured, functionally ordered, and stylish mansions of fifteenth-century England.

11. Town houses

England and Wales were essentially agricultural countries throughout the Middle Ages, with towns and industrial centres housing only a small proportion of the population. The definition of a town differs between historians and archaeologists but it should include the components of being a substantial community of several hundred or more people contributing to or making a living from trade or industry. The settlement would often be enclosed within walls or ditches and might be organised or trading under a charter. A few towns developed as urban communities during the eighth and ninth centuries (London, Hamwic, York), often in association with market places for trading, but such developments were hastened by the establishment of planned towns. Nearly seventy were founded in England and Wales by local lords between 1066 and 1130 (Carlisle, Durham, Shrewsbury), with a similar peak between 1190 and 1230 (Oxford, Cambridge). The bubonic plague that swept across the country in 1348, combined with the economic consequences of the Hundred Years' War, wrought major changes in British trading. Many towns went into decline (Lincoln, Winchelsea, York) while new centres prospered (Chipping Campden, Lavenham, Tiverton).

The principal unit of medieval urban land was the burgage, a narrow, elongated strip of land leased out for an annual rent. The burgages of York were laid out as early as the tenth century and those of Chester during the twelfth

Winchelsea, Sussex: Court House. The grid-like town of Winchelsea was established by Edward I between 1280 and 1290 after the port had been destroyed by the encroaching sea. This stone-built house was erected for Gervase Alard, the town's mayor, in 1295. It has lost an east wing and been much altered through its subsequent use as a prison, court house and museum. Thirty-three accessible undercrofts have survived in the town, mainly serving the Gascon wine trade.

century. Initially, the frontages were reasonably wide but, as building space became limited and commercial pressures grew to maximise the benefit of direct street access, subdivision was increasingly practised during the thirteenth and fourteenth centuries.

Architecturally, medieval town houses differed from countryside properties, not only as a consequence of space restrictions but principally because of their trading functions. However, continuous commercial activities, as well as domestic occupation, have been subject to such widespread changes of fortune over the centuries that few early houses still stand. Many were destroyed in the name of 'progress' during the nineteenth and twentieth centuries, abetted by town planners after the Second World War who were not interested in adequate recording or property analysis in their anxiety to sweep away bomb-damaged sites and replace them with sterile concrete streetscapes. The earliest standing structures are stone-built of the twelfth century, with thirty such houses in Canterbury recorded in the city's documents before 1200, but the thirteenth century marked a movement in favour of less expensive timber framing, which became the dominant material for all town houses until the advent of brick under the late Tudors.

STONE HOUSES

Early stone houses can be seen in Chester, King's Lynn, Lincoln, Norwich, Sandwich, Shrewsbury, Southampton and York. It is unfortunate that some of these have been given fictitious names (King John's Palace and Canute's Palace, Southampton; Moyse's Hall, Bury St Edmunds; Jew's House, Lincoln) when

Lincoln: Jew's House. The elaborate ground-floor entrance is mainly Norman, as is the buttress above containing the chimney of the fireplace serving the first-floor room. The upper window arches are also original, with the southernmost retaining much of its original form. The modernised interior retains three plain doorways.

155

Lincoln: Aaron's House. There was originally a chimney buttress above the entry door, as in the Jew's House. The first-floor Norman window was restored in 1878 after its discovery in pieces in a ground-floor recess. There is a fine barrel-vaulted cellar, reached from a stair outside the original rear doorway.

most of them were actually the houses of merchants or urban administrations. But, in contrast with most country houses, their occupiers usually lack clearly identifiable status. Furthermore, our perception of early towns is distorted by the absence of early timber houses as a consequence of rebuilding or total replacement.

Early stone houses were two-storeyed and followed the plan of first-floor accommodation over ground-floor rooms used for storage or commerce. The Treasurer's House in York (c.1080) and the Music House in King Street, Norwich (early twelfth century), are precocious survivals but the clearest examples are the two late Norman houses of affluent citizens in Lincoln. Aaron's House, Steep Hill, and the Jew's House, The Strait, are relatively complete, roofed, and still commercially occupied. The embellished ground-floor entrance led to two first-floor rooms with decorated windows and to the more important chamber heated by an enclosed fireplace. The ground-floor storage area may have been used as two shops or workshops from earliest times. The almost contemporary Moyse's Hall (c.1190), still dominating the market place at Bury St Edmunds, displays a similar two-room plan of residential chambers over vaulted undercrofts. Two or three centuries later, similar stone-built houses occur in Wales. Aberconwy House, Conwy, built in c.1420, has a timber hall and inner room over the commercially used stone ground floor. The Tudor Merchant's House of c.1500 at Tenby is equally narrow but three-storeyed, heated, and privy-protected on each floor.

Stone-built undercrofts might be built at street level or sunk partly below ground, with the latter predominating during the later Middle Ages. Often divided by columns that supported vaults, they survive far more frequently than the contemporary houses above them, but their distribution is irregular. They

156

are plentiful in Chester, Southampton, Winchester and London, suggesting they were a feature of coastal and river towns, but they are not found in Exeter, Salisbury or York. A few of those in Chester were probably built in the twelfth century but virtually all the twenty-five surviving cellars under the famous 'Rows' date from the late thirteenth century, many dendro-dated to the 1280s, spurred by its adoption by Edward I as a garrison town and centre for his castle-building programme in north Wales. Of these, five undercrofts are vaulted, with the remainder aisled with beams supporting timber and stone upper floors. It is likely that they were used for storing merchandise, with the raised ground floor serving a different commercial purpose leading to the split-level access. Some undercrofts are more elaborate than would be expected for storage (The Undercroft, Simnel Street, Southampton; 13 St Mary's Hill, Stamford). It is possible they were also used for display or as craft workshops rather than as stock rooms, or perhaps as taverns. Nearly all the seventy undercrofts in Norwich are brick-built, developed after 1350, with the majority of fifteenth-century date. Usually the structures above such undercrofts have been rebuilt but there is little doubt that they carried a superstructure used for commercial and residential purposes. This is more vividly demonstrated by Dragon Hall, Norwich (c.1430), where restoration has shown that Richard Toppes, a rich clothier, used the upper floor as a vast display area, divided into a showroom and a more private, opulent and heated section for privileged customers.

London was the one city with a substantial number of stone houses. This arose less from it being the most important and largest commercial entrepot in England than from its position next to the centre of administration, justice, parliament, and the monarchy at Westminster. Leading magnates, lay and ecclesiastical, needed a residential base close to the crown and government so that the area within the City and along the Strand as it extended towards Westminster was lined with stone houses, usually known as inns. They were on the grandest scale and are classic examples of *rus in urbe*, manor houses transferred wholesale to an urban environment. Virtually all these properties have been destroyed, though the ruined hall of the Bishops of Winchester in Southwark, the chapel of the Bishops of Ely in Holborn and the palace of the Archbishops of Canterbury in Lambeth are indicative of the scale and quality of such residences. Inns jostled with commercial properties in the City but even the house of the wealthy merchant Sir John Crosby in Bishopsgate could not withstand destruction for street development in 1905, except for the hall, a smaller version of its contemporary at Eltham Palace, which was re-erected on Chelsea Embankment. But London was not quite alone in grand houses, for status, self-esteem, and display were as redolent in medieval cities and towns as in the country. Wealthy merchants were responsible for developing Strangers' Hall, Norwich, into a late medieval courtyard mansion, paying for the late fourteenth-century hammer-beam roof at Balle's Place, Salisbury, and the tiled floors at Clifton House, King's Lynn, and William Canynge's house in Bristol, demolished for street widening in 1937.

TIMBER-FRAMED HOUSES

The majority of town houses were timber-framed as this form of construction was less expensive than stone. Since the 1960s a considerable body of foundation evidence has been identified of late Anglo-Saxon framed houses, shops and workshops, though sometimes there has been disagreement over its

London: the Bishop of Bath's Inn. This London episcopal house, set back from the river Thames in what is now Fleet Street, included an early fourteenth-century hall with porch. Hollar's drawing of 1646 shows that the offices were timber-framed with the kitchens to the left. Later buildings were added after the property had been acquired by the Earl of Arundel in 1549.

interpretation as above-ground buildings. But to the basic house elements previously discussed – hall, services and chamber – must now be added warehouse space and a shop. The configuration of these units in a confined space gradually led to four house types, of which two were of prime importance. The single-unit shop with no more than an unheated chamber above was at the lowest end of the scale (Lady Row, York, of 1315). The miniature manor house in a commercial setting – a separate entrance between shops to a small courtyard with the hall and apartments round it – was at the highest end of the scale (5–6 Market Place, Faversham). Between these two extremes come the majority of town houses.

The keynote in both circumstances was the position of the hall in relation to the street. It could either be parallel to the street or at right angles to it, with the layout of all the other rooms determined by this. In a house where the hall was parallel to the street the entry passage, services and chamber were in line with the hall, as occurred in so many manor houses. A variation on this type is the double parallel range, where the street is fronted by several shops (with rooms above), with a through passage to the hall and principal chamber at the rear.

Street frontage limitations and the pressure to maximise the return from burgage plots determined the second house type, where the hall was built at a right angle with its gable-end facing the street. Several houses of this type could be built on a single burgage plot with their line of jettied gables creating a repetitive but distinctive street façade. The hall and chamber would be positioned to the rear. This can be readily appreciated at 58 French Street, Southampton, where the shop has a chamber above, an open-to-the-roof hall in the middle, and two tiered chambers to the rear, all displayed today in furnished condition. The property also has separate street access to the undercroft and a jettied or projecting upper street frontage to gain more residential space – a marked feature of late medieval towns (Shrewsbury, Tewkesbury, York). A hall had the benefit of serving as a barrier between the property's commercial and domestic functions, but lighting such an apartment in a house of depth proved a continuing problem, leading to its elimination by the sixteenth century in favour of a well-lit upper room to the street or to the rear.

158

Southampton: Merchant's House, French Street. Restored and furnished in 1985 after bomb damage, this is one of the earliest surviving merchants' houses in England. Built in c.1290, it includes a vaulted cellar with a ground-floor shop fronting the hall, which is open to the roof. There is an inner room to the rear and there are two bedchambers at the front and back of the house. The property was probably used for storing and selling wine from Bordeaux, as well as general merchandise.

The variety of town-house plans and the diversity of room use is not surprising when they served so many different commercial purposes over two or more centuries, in addition to post-medieval adaptations and changes. We also need to know more about retail practices, shop fittings, and workshop facilities and outlets and to what extent they changed during the medieval period. In some instances the shop and the domestic areas are integrated. In others there is no intercommunication between the shop and the chamber above, with the more extensive domestic area suggesting independent retail tenancies. The study of town houses has developed only since the 1960s, so that the consequence of social and topographical constraints on urban building is only beginning to be appreciated,

Rye, Sussex. A line of timber-framed houses adjacent to the church with frontal jetties. They have not been dendro-dated but the thin timbers suggest later sixteenth-century frontages.

as are commercial pressures, workshop practices, and the growth of industrial centres in medieval England. But London was the only town that could compare with leading centres in France or Italy and only seventeen house fragments have survived centuries of post-medieval development. England's other leading towns, Bristol, Coventry, Norwich and York, were small in comparison and have few major survivals comparable to those in European cities such as Bruges, Ghent, and Lucca.

CATHEDRAL CLOSES

The residences built for the dignitaries of the nine secular cathedrals in England are the individual houses of a privileged community, wall-enclosed within a larger town circuit. These cathedral closes form the most compact group of medieval town houses to have survived, a contrasting environment to the urban community next to them. The houses surrounding the closes at Salisbury, Wells and Lincoln are the most extensive, with a lesser number of properties surviving at Chichester, Exeter and York, a few at Hereford and Lichfield, and none at St Paul's, London, after the great fire of 1666. The largest houses were those for the principal officials – the dean, chancellor, precentor and treasurer – followed by those of their deputies, with the remainder built for the canons and priests. Most of these houses have survived because they were built in stone and are still mainly ecclesiastically owned and occupied. Cathedral closes, therefore, are an institution and environment of unbroken continuity after eight hundred years. Because of its size, the diocese of York was also supported by three minsters at Beverley, Ripon, and Southwell, each with a church of cathedral-like scale surrounded by canons' houses comparable to those of the other cities, though in smaller numbers. All such houses were initially privately built, often bequeathed to the cathedral for use by succeeding officials, or deliberately built by the chapter from the end of the thirteenth

Salisbury: Cathedral Close. Built between 1258 and 1274, the hall of the Old Deanery has been restored to its early condition, displaying its original trussed rafter roof and the only thirteenth-century louvre framing in England.

Salisbury: Cathedral Close. King's House was originally built in the 1220s, at the same time as the cathedral opposite, as the house for the abbot of Sherborne, but its name was changed in the eighteenth century to commemorate the visits of James I. Its centre part essentially dates from the fifteenth century, when it comprised a hall open to the roof, parlour with chamber above, entry porch and kitchen to the side, all in flint rubble. The large windows were inserted in c.1600.

century onwards. They always stood near the cathedral, were set back from the road, but within the walled and gated enclosure that protected them from the morals, noise, and intrusiveness of the adjacent urban world.

As the cathedrals developed and expanded during the twelfth and thirteenth centuries, so did the number of clergy, with their organisational structure reaching its peak during the fourteenth century; there were 110 clergy at the relatively small cathedral of Exeter in 1337 and 130 clergy at Salisbury in 1390. A close was therefore a self-contained, self-governing and hierarchical unit, a smaller version of a baronial household, and, like them, it became more complex during the later thirteenth century and the first half of the fourteenth. This was therefore the great age of cathedral close development. The larger houses were those of the four principal officials, who altered and developed them in the same way that the bishops did with their palaces. The flint-built deanery of 1258–74 at Salisbury has a hall, 50 feet by 31 feet (15.2 by 9.4 metres), as large as that of a manor house. It had three service doorways, a central hearth, louvre, dais, gabled side windows and the original trussed rafter roof. The hall of the deanery at Wells is a late Tudor replacement but this essentially late fifteenth-century double-courtyard residence retains its gatehouse and highly decorated suite of private and guest apartments added by Dean Gunthorpe in c.1480. The hall of the chancellor's imposing residence of c.1320 at Lincoln divided the property into two courts and, though it no longer survives, the remainder of this house does, expanded in brick by Bishop Russell (1480–94), who similarly worked at Buckden Palace. In contrast with the adjacent town houses, these properties have the same components as a country

161

Wells, Somerset: Bishop's Palace. The palace was enclosed with embattled walls and a gatehouse by Bishop Ralph in 1340. These fortifications look menacing but the walls lack mid defensive towers, the moat is shallow, and the gatehouse is a multi-lodging block of seven independent units. This development was not only an assertion of power and authority but encompasses a contemporary pictorial and landscaping element.

manor house – a large hall, great chamber, chapel, guest room, kitchen and garden, with those of the deputy officers and senior canons being far smaller versions. Though the Treasurer's House at York is a seventeenth-century rebuilding, it has the benefit of being open to the public to give a vivid impression of the environment necessary for dispensing lavish hospitality in a cathedral precinct.

COMMUNAL BUILDINGS

The growth of towns in the thirteenth and fourteenth centuries and the organisation of trade guilds went hand in hand, so that the majority of guildhalls that survive were built between *c.*1350 and 1550. Most of them were

Norton St Philip, Somerset: George Inn. This late fourteenth-century inn was remodelled in stages during the fifteenth century. The main range dates from 1431 with a rebuilt street front of two overhanging jetties. Internally, the earlier hall was fully opened to the roof with frontal galleries at first- and second-floor levels. Both upper levels were completely floored in the sixteenth century.

Norton St Philip: George Inn. The oldest part of the inn is its rear wall of c.1370–1400, three-storeyed and entirely stone-built, consisting of a hall with a top-floor dormitory. The stair turret was added in 1431 to serve the newly created galleries to the timber-framed frontage. The courtyard range (left) is also fifteenth-century.

constructed in the eastern part of the country, reflecting that region's greater prosperity (King's Lynn, Lavenham, Norwich). However, the finest medieval example is St Mary's Hall, Coventry, where the first-floor hall of c.1394–9 above a slightly earlier undercroft was modelled on the contemporary great hall at Kenilworth Castle. Guildhall development stemmed from the planning of private houses, which were frequently gifted to the guild by a wealthy citizen, as at Great Yarmouth and the Merchant Taylors' Hall, London. Despite enlargement or adaptation, the majority of guildhalls continued to reflect the basic medieval domestic components of hall, parlour, kitchen, and garden. Many prosperous guilds subsequently built their own premises (Lavenham, York, London) but less wealthy guilds would often unite to develop a common structure, as at Warwick (1383–c.1500).

Inns were also modelled on domestic houses, in general, and town houses in particular. The word 'inn' derives from the grand houses built in London and Southwark that came to be let out to travellers during the sixteenth century and readily evolved into totally commercial enterprises. The earliest properties specially built for this purpose all date from the fifteenth century, including the galleried New Inn, Gloucester (c.1440), the White Hart, Newark (1460s), the Angel, Grantham (1480s), and the George, Glastonbury (c.1480). They reflect the principal components of town house planning but with some important modifications, including a preference for ranges built round a courtyard, varied hall sizes, a multiplicity of chambers, and gallery access to the upper rooms.

163

12. Yeoman and peasant houses

Modern research has revealed far more gradations of medieval agrarian society and greater fluidity than had been previously considered. Even so, documentation is patchy and often lacks the detailing that historians would like, making it difficult to bring the same precision to 'yeoman' and 'peasant' as to people of higher social status. Any assessment of standing will be based on land holding and that, in turn, depends on whether it is upland or lowland, on its economic location, the soil quality, and the agrarian structure of the area. The wealthiest regions of England and Wales lay east and south of a line from York to Bristol while the poorest were the far north, central Wales and south-west England. This contributed to differences in house form and scale, but so did the dramatic change in the economy of peasant society following the Black Death of 1348–9, which reduced the population of about 4.5 million by almost a half. The impact was a gradual build-up to a fundamental agrarian change between about 1370 and 1430 with a shift from arable to pastoral farming. Accelerated by the partial success of the Peasants' Revolt of 1381, servile obligations to a manorial lord were gradually replaced by rent tenancies, and peasant holdings grew larger through amalgamation, while their living standards rose over the next two or three generations. Peasant tenure and landholding were totally reshaped by the second quarter of the fifteenth century and as a consequence two strata of society evolved.

The majority of the population – at least 80 per cent – were low-income rural cultivators with the right to manage their own property, which varied from an

This timber-framed house of 1480–1520 a few miles south-east of Maidstone, Kent, was possibly built for a wealthy yeoman or minor gentry. It had a central hall open to the roof, with end wings built in line under a single roof span. However, the upper end bays were jettied to the front (and sides) to project forward of the hall so that it stands recessed at the upper level. Houses of this type are known as 'Wealden' houses, as they are numerous in the Weald region. Visually, they are the most attractive of the many early yeoman-type houses in England and Wales.

164

Mill Farm Cottage near Mapledurham, Oxfordshire, dendro-dated to c.1335, is a single-storey, timber-framed building of three bays. It was made up of a two-bay hall with an arch-braced central truss (perhaps to give it dignity) and an inner room. The house is now thatched and was probably always so, though attic rooms were added in the nineteenth century. It was possibly of peasant origin, but the precise financial and social standing of its builder is unclear.

acre or two to thirty or more. However, during the early fourteenth century, if not before, the more affluent were replacing their labour service with rental and were increasingly involved in hiring labour and selling surplus produce, a practice which dramatically increased after the Black Death. It was they who tended to become the peasant aristocracy – the yeoman class. Holding 50 acres or more and possibly a flock of sheep, they straddled the divide between gentry and peasantry.

This gradual increase in the freedom and spending power of the rural population at all levels extended as much to their houses as to their higher standards of living. As a consequence, extensive research since the 1950s has shown that England and Wales retain an extremely wide span of yeoman and peasant housing from the later Middle Ages. We are not considering one or two hundred properties but a figure closer to two or three thousand, which grows even larger if the sub-medieval period to about 1600 is taken into consideration.

The subject has become a separate area of study with a society established in 1952, the Vernacular Architecture Group, devoted to the study of lesser traditional buildings. The consideration of vernacular buildings includes cottages, farmhouses, barns and the structures associated with farm activities and those of modest industrial enterprises before the advent of factories. They are traditional rather than socially aspirational, unpretentious rather than imposing, and utilitarian rather than decorative in character. The difference between greater or polite houses and peasant or vernacular houses is obvious at the extremes, but it is one of degree rather than absolutes in between. But during the Middle Ages in particular, there was one further difference, which depended on its permanence. The houses we have been considering in this book were intended to stand for generations, but many peasant properties and associated farm buildings were far more temporary in their materials and structure. Most of these farm units and outhouses have been all but lost until revealed during archaeological or architectural explorations.

The dating of vernacular buildings can be a challenge but the development of dendrochronology since the late 1960s has brought much greater precision to this aspect of the subject. In a study of 450 houses in Kent built before 1540, fifty-three were tree-ring dated. Only three were earlier than the Black Death and they were of manorial status. There seems to have been a building gap during the mid fourteenth century until the 1370s, when the fifty dated houses begin and continue fairly evenly spread across the next hundred and seventy years. Since 1984 the Vernacular Architecture Group journal has included a comprehensive listing and brief analysis of all dendrochronological assessments undertaken across England and Wales during the previous year. From 1996, this has also included those carried out for English Heritage.

A subject that spans the thirteenth to the nineteenth centuries warrants separate treatment, particularly as it is subject to many regional variations of structure and materials. So far, only one book has covered the subject, Eric Mercer's *English Vernacular Houses* (1975) and that now needs substantial revision. Otherwise, surveys tend to be county-based rather than regional, such as those by Sarah Pearson for Kent (1994), Edward Roberts for Hampshire (2003), Madge Moran for Shropshire (2004) and Richard Suggett for Radnorshire (2005). The overall picture for yeoman and peasant housing is therefore patchy. Even so, it has revealed that the later Middle Ages was not a period of continuous growth and development between 1350 and 1500 but one of varied fortune in different parts of the country. Whereas peasant houses in Suffolk, Essex and Kent increased in number in line with the area's prosperity, there is an almost total absence of them in other development areas such as West Yorkshire during the late fifteenth century. The north of England, in particular, suffered from severe economic depression throughout the mid fifteenth century. We therefore have a paradox across the country and the period. On the one hand, many long-established towns were in decline, rents were falling and deserted villages were becoming a feature of the landscape, whereas other areas enjoyed higher wages, cheaper land and localised prosperity. While farming entrepreneurs or those supporting a trade or profession invested in a new house, others suffered penury, with their houses falling down or abandoned. Until more regional studies on peasant properties have been completed with precision about ownership and financial standing, then it will not be possible to relate the pattern of fluctuating economic fortune with the growing body of evidence indicative of architectural prosperity for some, while others at the same lower social level suffered misfortune.

13. Further reading

GENERAL

The volumes of *The Buildings of England* series by Nikolaus Pevsner are invaluable introductions to individual counties and their buildings, but they are better in the revised and expanded second editions so far as medieval houses are concerned. The companion series *The Buildings of Wales* is equally useful. Most house guides are superficial or disgraceful except those of English Heritage, Cadw, and recent National Trust handbooks. The weekly magazine *Country Life* has a long-established reputation for well-illustrated and researched articles on individual houses. Many of them have been brought together in edited volumes by Avray Tipping, Christopher Hussey and more recent architectural editors.

BUILDING RECORDS

The first chapter of Jane Grenville's *Medieval Housing* (1997) briefly covers the developing field of archaeological and scientific sources, while the introduction to John Harvey's *English Medieval Architects* (second edition 1984) assesses the documentary aspects. Licences to crenellate will be covered shortly in a book by Charles Coulson. John Leland's *Itinerary* was edited by L. T. Smith (1906–10) with a modern English version arranged by counties by John Chandler (1993).

ARCHITECTURAL DEVELOPMENT

The first half of Maurice Barley *Houses and History* (1986) covers the broad span of English housing from Anglo-Saxon to Tudor times, as does Jane Grenville's volume of 1997 mentioned above. T. H. Turner and J. H. Parker

Shute, Devon. An unusual survival, the two-storey kitchen (left) and services with staff rooms above of a trophy house built by Sir William Bonville in the 1430s. The photograph is taken from the site of the hall which was pulled down in the 1560s when the large windows were inserted (right).

167

Some Account of Domestic Architecture of the Middle Ages (three volumes, 1851–9) is still valuable, particularly for the house descriptions and illustrations before Victorian and subsequent alterations.

For all royal works, the first two volumes covering the Middle Ages in the series *The History of the King's Works*, edited by H. M. Colvin (1963), are an essential resource. Michael Thompson *The Medieval Hall* (1995) is a broad but old-fashioned review. The same author's *Medieval Bishops' Houses in England and Wales* (1998) is more useful.

For houses of the twelfth century, Margaret Wood on Norman domestic architecture in *Archaeological Journal* volume 92 (1935) needs revising, as does her subsequent volume on thirteenth-century houses, a supplement to *Archaeological Journal* volume 105 (1950). Some of the material was included in her architecturally-determined volume *The English Medieval House* (1965). The residences of the fourteenth and fifteenth centuries are covered in the three volumes by Anthony Emery *Greater Medieval Houses of England and Wales: 1300–1500* (1996–2006). The years preceding the Reformation, which marks the close of the Middle Ages, are covered in the early chapters of Maurice Howard *The Early Tudor Country House* (1987) and Nicholas Cooper *Houses of the Gentry: 1480–1680* (1999).

BUILDING MATERIALS

Alec Clifton-Taylor *The Pattern of English Building* (fourth edition 1987) is a well-written, enthusiastic survey concentrating on domestic architecture. More specialist works include *Stone: Quarrying and Building AD 43–1525*, edited by D. Parsons (1990), A. Clifton-Taylor and A. S. Ireson *English Stone Building* (second edition 1994), and Jane Wight *Brick Building in England from the Middle Ages to 1550* (1972). Cecil Hewett *English Historic Carpentry* (1980) is supplemented by *Regional Variation in Timber-Framed Building in England and Wales down to 1550*, edited by D. F. Stenning and D. D. Andrews (1998). N. W. Alcock *et al*, *Recording Timber-framed Buildings: An Illustrated Glossary* (2004) is a major source for standard terms and descriptions. All the subjects are also covered in *English Medieval Industries* edited by J. Blair and N. Ramsey (1991).

CONTENTS AND FURNISHINGS

The subject still awaits an overview. The most up-to-date essays are in two exhibition catalogues: *The Age of Chivalry*, edited by J. Alexander and P. Binski (1987), covering art from 1200 to 1400, and *Gothic*, edited by R. Marks and P. Williamson (2003), celebrating English art from 1400 to 1547. Earlier studies are those in the Oxford History series, *English Art 1216–1307* by Peter Brieger (1957) and *English Art 1307–1461* by Joan Evans (1949). Charles Kightly *Living Rooms: Interior Decoration in Wales 400–1960* (2005) is a well-illustrated account.

POLITICAL AND SOCIAL HISTORY

Books on political, social and economic history are legion. Three volumes in the New Oxford History of England series giving current overviews are Robert Bartlett *England under the Norman and Angevin Kings 1075–1225* (2004), Michael Prestwich *Plantagenet England 1225–1360* (2005) and Gerald Harriss *Shaping the Nation: England 1360–1461* (2005). All three volumes include critical bibliographies pointing to more specialised fields of study, such as Chris Given-Wilson *English Nobility in the Late Middle Ages* (1987) and E. B. Fryde *Peasants and Landlords in Later Medieval England* (1996).

COMPARATIVE RESIDENCES

J. Patrick Greene *Medieval Monasteries* (1992) gives an archaeological review of the subject, as does Glyn Coppack *Abbeys and Priories* (1990). Colin Platt *The Abbeys and Priories of Medieval England* (1984) gives a historian's perspective but a broad architectural study is needed. *Vicars Choral at English Cathedrals*, edited by R. Hall and D. Stocker (2005), is an in-depth study. Among the volumes on the colleges at Oxford and Cambridge are those by the Royal Commission on Historical Monuments *City of Oxford* (1939) and *City of Cambridge* (1959). Geoffrey Tyack *Oxford: An Architectural Guide* (1998) and Tim Rawle *Cambridge: Architecture* (1985) are shorter surveys. The radical new approach to castle studies is exemplified by Matthew Johnson *Behind the Castle Gate* (2002) and by Robert Liddiard *Castles in Context* (2005).

TOWN HOUSES

W. A. Pantin's essay 'Medieval English town-house plans' in *Medieval Archaeology* volumes 6–7 (1962–3) is still a valuable source, while Anthony Quiney *Town Houses of Medieval Britain* (2003) is a richly illustrated historical and architectural survey. John Schofield and Alan Vince assess the archaeological evidence in *Medieval Towns* (second edition 2003) while John Schofield *Medieval London Houses* (1995) is the summation of extensive research in the metropolis, principally during the last fifty years.

YEOMEN AND PEASANTRY

Apart from Eric Mercer's overview *English Vernacular Houses* (1975) and the county surveys mentioned in the text, Christopher Dyer *Standards of Living in the Late Middle Ages* (1985) is a pioneering survey, with the same author giving a synthesis of the documentary evidence from 1200 to 1500 in *Medieval Archaeology* volume 30 (1986). This has been extended by excavated evidence summarised by Mark Gardiner in the same journal, volume 44 (2000).

Wells: The Deanery. Built round a small quadrangle, the core of the buttressed range (left) is thirteenth-century (with windows of 1690–1700). The house was exuberantly remodelled in c.1480 by Dean Gunthorpe, who added the entry gateway and terraced forecourt.

169

14. Houses and comparable buildings open to the public

Details of all properties in the United Kingdom open to the public are given in Hudson's annual publication *Historic Houses and Gardens* (www.hudsonsguide.co.uk). The following is a selection of the more important medieval houses. Details of houses in the care of the National Trust (NT), English Heritage (EH) or Cadw can be found on the respective websites of those organisations: www.nationaltrust.org.uk; www.english-heritage.org.uk; www.cadw.wales.gov.uk

ENGLAND
BERKSHIRE
Windsor Castle, Windsor SL4 1NJ. Telephone: 01753 831118 (infoline). Website: www.royalcollection.org.uk

CAMBRIDGESHIRE
Buckden Palace, High Street, Buckden, St Neots PE19 5TA. Telephone: 01480 810344. Website: www.fobt.fsnet.co.uk

Hemingford Grey Manor, Hemingford Grey, Huntingdon PE28 9BN. Telephone: 01480 463134. Website: www.greenknowe.co.uk

Longthorpe Tower (EH), Longthorpe, Peterborough PE1 1HA. Telephone: 01799 522842.

CHESHIRE
Tatton Park Old Hall (NT), Knutsford WA16 6QN. Telephone: 01625 534400. Website: www.tattonpark.org.uk

CORNWALL
Cotehele (NT), St Dominick, near Saltash PL12 6TA. Telephone: 01579 351346.

Penhallam Manor (EH).

CUMBRIA
Sizergh Castle (NT), Sizergh, near Kendal LA8 8AE. Telephone: 01539 560951.

DERBYSHIRE
Haddon Hall, Bakewell DE45 1LA. Telephone: 01629 812855. Website: www.haddonhall.co.uk

Wingfield Manor (EH), South Wingfield DE55 7NH. Telephone: 01773 832060.

DEVON
Bradley Manor (NT), Newton Abbot TQ12 6BN. Telephone: 01626 354513.

Compton Castle (NT), Marldon, Paignton TQ3 1TA. Telephone: 01803 842382.

Dartington Hall, Totnes TQ9 6EL. Telephone: 01803 847100. Website: www.dartingtonhall.org.uk; www.dartingtonhall.com

Shute Barton (NT), Shute, near Axminster EX13 7PT. Telephone: 01297 34692.

DORSET
Athelhampton Hall, Athelhampton, Dorchester DT2 7LG. Telephone: 01305 848363. Website: www.athelhampton.co.uk

Fiddleford Manor (EH), Sturminster Newton.

COUNTY DURHAM
Bishop Auckland Castle, Bishop Auckland DL14 7NR. Telephone: 01388 601627. Website: www.auckland-castle.co.uk

Raby Castle, Staindrop, Darlington DL2 3AH. Telephone: 01833 660202. Website: www.rabycastle.com

ESSEX
Southchurch Hall, Southchurch Hall Close, Southend-on-Sea, Essex. Telephone: 01702 467671. Website: www.southendmuseums.co.uk

HAMPSHIRE
Bishop's Waltham Palace (EH), Bishop's Waltham SO32 1DH. Telephone: 01489 892460.
The Great Hall, The Castle, Winchester. Telephone: 01962 846476. Website: www.hants.gov.uk/greathall

KENT
Ightham Mote (NT), Mote Road, Ivy Hatch, Sevenoaks TN15 0NT. Telephone: 01732 810378.
Old Soar Manor (NT), Plaxtol, Borough Green TN15 0QX. Telephone: 01732 810378.
Penshurst Place and Gardens, Penshurst TN11 8DG. Telephone: 01892 870307. Website: www.penshurstplace.com
Temple Manor, Strood. Telephone: 01634 843666.
  Website: www.medway.gov.uk/index/leisure/tourism

LANCASHIRE
Rufford Old Hall (NT), 200 Liverpool Road, Rufford, near Ormskirk L40 1SG. Telephone: 01704 821254.
Smithills Hall, Smithills Dean Road, Bolton BL1 7NP. Telephone: 01204 332377. Website: www.boltonmuseums.org.uk
Warton Old Rectory (EH), Warton, near Carnforth.

LEICESTERSHIRE
Ashby de la Zouch Castle (EH), Ashby de la Zouch LE65 1BR. Telephone: 01530 413343.
Donnington le Heath Manor House, Manor Road, Donington-le-Heath, Coalville LE67 2FW. Telephone: 01530 831259.
  Website: www.leics.gov.uk/index/community/museums
Kirby Muxloe Castle (EH), Kirby Muxloe LE9 9MD. Telephone: 0116 238 6886.

LINCOLNSHIRE
Bishop's Palace (EH), Lincoln LN2 1PU. Telephone: 01522 527468.
Gainsborough Old Hall (EH), Gainsborough DN21 2NB. Telephone: 01427 612669.
  Website: www.gainsborougholdhall.co.uk
Tattershall Castle (NT), Tattershall, Lincoln LN4 4LR. Telephone: 01526 342543.

LONDON
Eltham Palace, Court Yard, Eltham SE9 5QE. Telephone: 020 8294 2548. Website: www.elthampalace.org.uk
Westminster Hall and Jewel Tower, Westminster SW1A 0AA. Telephone: 020 7219 4272 or 020 7222 2219 (Jewel Tower). Website: www.parliament.uk/works

NORTHAMPTONSHIRE
Prebendal Manor House, Nassington, near Peterborough PE8 6QG. Telephone: 01780 782575. Website: www.prebendal-manor.co.uk

NORTHUMBERLAND
Aydon Castle (EH), Aydon, near Corbridge NE45 5PJ. Telephone: 01434 632450.
Belsay Castle (EH), Belsay NE20 0DX. Telephone: 01661 881636.

OXFORDSHIRE
Broughton Castle, Banbury OX15 5EB. Telephone: 01295 276070. Website: www.broughtoncastle.com

Minster Lovell Hall (EH), Minster Lovell.

Stonor Park, Henley-on-Thames RG9 6HF. Telephone: 01491 638587. Website: www.stonor.com

RUTLAND

Lyddington Bede House (EH), Lyddington LE15 9LZ. Telephone: 01572 822438.

Oakham Castle, Market Place, Oakham LE15 6DX. Telephone: 01572 758440. Website: www.rutland.gov.uk/castle

SHROPSHIRE

Acton Burnell Castle (EH), Acton Burnell.

Ludlow Castle, Castle Square, Ludlow SY8 1AY. Telephone: 01584 873356. Website: www.ludlowcastle.com

Stokesay Castle (EH), Stokesay. Telephone: 01588 672554.

SOMERSET

Bishop's Palace, Wells BA5 2PD. Telephone: 01749 678691. Website: www.bishopspalacewells.co.uk

Clevedon Court (NT), Tickenham Road, Clevedon BS21 6QU. Telephone: 01275 872257.

Treasurer's House (NT), Martock TA12 6JL. Telephone: 01935 825015.

SUSSEX

Great Dixter, Northiam, Rye TN31 6PH. Telephone: 01797 252878. Website: www.greatdixter.co.uk

Herstmonceux Castle, Hailsham BN27 1RN. Telephone: 01323 833816. Website: www.herstmonceux-castle.com

WARWICKSHIRE

Baddesley Clinton (NT), Rising Lane, Baddesley Clinton Village, Knowle, Solihull B93 0DQ. Telephone: 01564 783294.

Kenilworth Castle, Castle Green, Kenilworth CV8 1NE. Telephone: 01926 852078. Website: www.english-heritage.org.uk/kenilworthcastle

WILTSHIRE

Great Chalfield Manor (NT), near Melksham SN12 8NH. Telephone: 01225 782239.

Wardour Castle (EH), near Tisbury SP3 6RR. Telephone: 01747 870487.

YORKSHIRE

Bolton Castle, Castle Bolton, near Leyburn DL8 4ET. Telephone: 01969 623981. Website: www.boltoncastle.com

Burton Agnes Hall, Burton Agnes, Driffield YO25 0ND. Telephone: 01262 490324. Website: www.burton-agnes.co.uk

Markenfield Hall, Ripon HG4 3AD. Telephone: 01765 692303. Website: www.markenfield.com

Spofforth Castle (EH), Spofforth, near Harrogate.

WALES

Bishop's Palace (Cadw), Lamphey, Pembrokeshire SA71 5NT. Telephone: 01646 672224.

Bishop's Palace (Cadw), St David's, Pembrokeshire SA62 6PE. Telephone: 01437 720517.

Penarth-fawr, Chwilog, Pwllheli, Gwynedd LL53 6PR. Telephone: 01766 810880. Website: www.gwynedd.gov.uk

Raglan Castle (Cadw), Raglan, Monmouthshire NP15 2BT. Telephone: 01291 690228.

Tretower Court (Cadw), Crickhowell, Powys NP8 1RF. Telephone: 01874 730279.

Weobley Castle (Cadw), Llanrhidian, Swansea, Glamorgan SA3 1HB. Telephone: 01792 390012.

COMPARABLE BUILDINGS

CHANTRY PRIESTS

St William's College, 4-5 College Street, York YO1 7JF. Telephone: 01904 557216. Website: www.yorkminster.org

Stoke sub Hamdon Priory (NT), North Street, Stoke sub Hamdon, Somerset TA4 6QP. Telephone: 01935 823289.

COLLEGES

Many of the colleges at Oxford and Cambridge are open to the public at selected times.

GUILDHALLS

The Leicester Guildhall, Guildhall Lane, Leicester LE1 5FQ. Telephone: 0116 253 2569. Website: www.leicestermuseums.ac.uk

Lord Leycester Hospital, High Street, Warwick CV34 4BH. Telephone: 01926 491422. Website: www.warwick-uk.co.uk/places-of-interest.asp

St George's Hall, 29 King Street, King's Lynn, Norfolk PE30 1HA. Telephone: 01553 764864. Website: www.kingslynnarts.co.uk/guildhall.html

St Mary's Hall, Bayley Lane, Coventry CV1 5RR. Telephone: 024 7683 3328. Website: www.coventry.gov.uk

MONASTIC LODGINGS

Battle Abbey (EH), Battle, Sussex TN33 0AD. Telephone: 01424 773792. Website: www.english-heritage.org.uk/battleabbey

Castle Acre Priory (EH), Castle Acre, Norfolk PE32 2XD. Telephone: 01760 755394.

Denny Abbey, Ely Road, Waterbeach, Cambridge CB5 9PQ. Telephone: 01223 860988. Website: www.dennyfarmlandmuseum.org.uk

Forde Abbey, Chard, Somerset TA20 4LU. Telephone: 01460 220231. Website: www.fordeabbey.co.uk

Muchelney Abbey (EH), Muchelney, Somerset TA10 0DQ. Telephone: 01458 250664.

TOWN HOUSES

Aberconwy House (NT), Castle Street, Conwy LL32 8AY. Telephone: 01492 592246.

Dragon Hall, 115-123 King Street, Norwich, Norfolk NR1 1QE. Telephone: 01603 663922. Website: www.dragonhall.org

Glastonbury Tribunal, 9 High Street, Glastonbury, Somerset BA6 9DP. Telephone: 01458 832954. Website: www.glastonburytic.co.uk

Medieval Merchant's House (EH), Southampton, Hampshire SO1 0AT. Telephone: 023 8022 1503.

Tudor Merchant's House (NT), Quay Hill, Tenby, Pembrokeshire SA70 7BX. Telephone: 01834 842279.

VERNACULAR HOUSES

Some of the most accessible vernacular houses are displayed in open-air museums such as:

Avoncroft Museum of Historic Buildings, Stoke Heath, Bromsgrove, Worcestershire B60 4JR. Telephone: 01527 831363. Website: www.avoncroft.org.uk

Ryedale Folk Museum, Hutton le Hole, Yorkshire YO62 6UA. Telephone: 01751 417367. Website: www.ryedalefolkmuseum.co.uk

St Fagans: National History Museum, St Fagans, Cardiff CF5 6XB. Telephone: 029 2057 3500. Website: www.museumwales.ac.uk

Weald & Downland Open Air Museum, Singleton, Chichester, West Sussex PO18 0EU. Telephone: 01243 811363. Website: www.wealddown.co.uk

Index

Page numbers in italic refer to illustrations

Oxford 10, 65, 90, 130, 141, 154; All Souls College 90; Magdalen College *152*, 153, *153*; Merton College 85; New College 32, 64, 66, 86, 90, 150-3, *150*

Padley Hall, Derbyshire 49

Paull Holme, Yorkshire 103

Peasant houses 7, 164-6

Peasants' Revolt (1381) 164

Penallt, Carmarthenshire 104

Penhallam Manor, Cornwall 65

Penrith Castle, Cumbria 102

Penshurst Place, Kent 12, 18, *47*, *48*, 49, 51, 56, 59, *60*, *80*, 87, 90, *90*, 92, 109, 111, *111*, 112

Pevensey Castle, Sussex 112

Plaxtol, Kent: Old Soar 39, *39*, 43, 55, *55*, 62

Political developments 7, 95-117

Pontefract Castle, Yorkshire 118

Portchester Castle, Hampshire *8*, 32, 72, 112

Preston Patrick Hall, Cumbria 56

Pulteney, Sir John 12, *47*, 109

Pwllheli, Gwynedd: Penarth-fawr 105

Queenborough Castle, Kent 110, 112

Raby Castle, Co. Durham 12, 66, 91, *126*, 127, 142

Raglan Castle, Monmouthshire 6, *83*, 84, 113, 114-16, *114*, 135

Ragley Castle, Warwickshire 13

Repton Priory, Derbyshire 79

Rey Manor, Norfolk 15

Richard II 25, 67, 123

Richmond Castle, Yorkshire 32, 33, 113

Richmond Palace, Surrey 79

Rievaulx Abbey, Yorkshire 142

Ripon, Yorkshire 160

Rochester Castle, Kent 110

Rotherfield Greys, Oxfordshire 12

Rufford Old Hall, Lancashire 52, 53

Rycote House, Oxfordshire 63

Rye, Sussex: Church Square *159*

Rye House, Hertfordshire 12, 78, 109

St David's Palace, Pembrokeshire 32, 107, *107*

St George-super-Ely, Glamorgan: Castle Farm 104

Salisbury, Wiltshire 157, 160, 161; Balle's Place 157; King's House *161*; Old Deanery 55, 86, *160*, 161

Salmestone Grange, Kent 146

Saltford Manor, Somerset 30

Saltwood Castle, Kent 93, 110, 112

Samlesbury Hall, Lancashire 53

Sampford Peverell, Devon: Old Rectory 150

Sandal Castle, Yorkshire 118

Sandwich, Kent 155

Savoy Palace, London 8, 109

Scotney Castle, Kent 67, 110, 112

Sheen Palace, Surrey 15, 69, 78, 81, 132

Shelton Hall, Norfolk 128

Sherborne Abbey, Dorset 142

Sheriff Hutton Castle, Yorkshire 12, 67, 127

Shibden Hall, Yorkshire 52

Shortflatt Tower, Northumberland 101, 102

Shrewsbury, Shropshire 154, 155, 158

Shute, Devon *167*

Sizergh Castle, Cumbria 84

Slough, Berkshire: Upton Court 56

Social developments 7, 118-40

South Kyme Tower, Lincolnshire *132*

South Witham, Lincolnshire 148

South Wraxall Manor, Wiltshire 51, 70

Southampton, Hampshire 155, 157; Castle 110; Merchant's House, French Street 158, *159*

Southwark, London 163

Southwell, Nottinghamshire 160; Palace *66*, 67

Spofforth Castle, Yorkshire *13*

Stafford Castle 9, 109

Stamford, Lincolnshire 157; Castle 118

Stanton Harcourt Manor House, Oxfordshire 49, 64

Steeton Hall, Yorkshire 65, 84, *84*, 145

Stoke sub Hamdon Priory, Somerset *148*

Stokesay Castle, Shropshire 6, 43, *43*, *44*, 45, *45*, 51, 64, 77, 81, 86, 131, *131*

Stonor Park, Oxfordshire 56, 80

Stonyhurst College, Lancashire 91

Stourton House, Wiltshire 15, 109, 139

Strood, Kent: Temple Manor 41, 148

Sudeley Castle, Gloucestershire 13, 18, *18*, 20, 69, 109, *134*, 135, 139, *139*

Sulgrave Manor, Northamptonshire 22, *22*

Tattershall Castle, Lincolnshire 10, 50,

52, 77-8, *77*, 83, *92*, 113, 116, 132-3, *132*

Temple Balsall, Warwickshire 148

Tenby, Pembrokeshire: Tudor Merchant's House 156

Tewkesbury, Gloucestershire 158

Thame Park, Oxfordshire 86

Thornage Hall, Norfolk 72

Thornbury Castle, Gloucestershire *16*, 17, 86, 122, 123, 131, 133, 135, 139-40, *140*

Thornhill Lees Hall, Yorkshire 52

Thornton Abbey, Lincolnshire 77, 145

Tickenham Court, Somerset 51

Tiptofts Manor, Essex 40-1, 56

Tisbury, Wiltshire: Place Farm 146

Tiverton, Devon 154

Tonford Manor, Kent 129

Town houses 7, 154-63

Towneley Hall, Lancashire 91

Treago Castle, Herefordshire 69, 139

Trent, Dorset: The Chantry 150

Tretower, Powys: Castle *105*; Court 65, 93, 105, *106*

Tutbury Castle, Staffordshire 8, 113, 118, 134

Upton Court, Slough, Berkshire 56

Valle Crucis Abbey, Denbighshire 142

Vyne, The, Basingstoke, Hampshire 62, 86

Wardour Castle, Wiltshire 131

Warkworth Castle, Northumberland 12, *19*, 84, 101, 102, 131

Warnford Manor, Hampshire 35

Wars of the Roses 112-17

Warwick: Castle 6, 113, 116-17, *116*; Guildhall (Lord Leycester's Hospital) 163

Watton Priory, Yorkshire 143

Wealden houses *164*

Weare Giffard Hall, Devon 91

Wells, Somerset 160; Bishop's Palace 32, 35, 37, *38*, 53, *54*, 86, *162*; The Deanery 70, 161, *169*; Vicars' Close *146*, 147

Wenlock Priory, Shropshire 88, 143

Weobley Castle, Glamorgan 104

Weoley Castle, Birmingham 11, *17*, 64

West Bower Manor, Somerset 65

West Bromwich Manor House, Staffordshire 52, 63, 82, 122

Westminster, London: Abbey 89; Palace 23, *23*, 25, 33, 56, 88, 124

Wetheral Priory, Cumbria 145

Whittington Castle, Shropshire 93

Wickham Court, Kent 15

Wigmore, Herefordshire: Abbey 142; Castle 118

William II 25

Winchelsea, Sussex 154; Court House *154*

Winchester, Bishops of 25, 110, 150-3

Winchester, Hampshire 157; Castle Hall 33, 34, 37, 80, 90, 93; College 16, 32, 66, 86, 90, 141, 150, 151-3, *151*; Pilgrims' Hall 56; St Cross Hospital 152; Wolvesey Palace 25, 27, 110

Winchester House, London 67

Windsor Castle, Berkshire 32, 64, 66, 81, 87, *108*, 109, 123, 125, 127, 128, 130, 148, 151, 152

Wingfield Manor, Derbyshire 10, 32, 49, 51, 52, 62, 64, *68*, 69, *69*, 81, 83, 88, 120, *120*, *121*, 123, 131, 132-3, *133*, 134, 137, 138, 142, 152

Wolvesey Palace, Winchester 25, 27, 110

Wonston Old House, Hampshire 64

Woodlands Manor, Wiltshire 62

Woodmanton, Worcestershire 12

Woodsford Castle, Dorset 11, *12*

Woodstock Palace, Oxfordshire 86, 124

Worcester: Commandery 86

Worcester, William 15

Workington Hall, Cumbria 69

Wotton-under-Edge Manor, Gloucestershire 118

Wressle Castle, Yorkshire 12, 15, 50, 67, 127, *127*

Wye College, Kent 147, 148

Wykeham, Bishop William 32, 150-3

Yate Court, Gloucestershire 12, 118

Yeavering Palace, Northumberland 21

Yelford Manor, Oxfordshire 75

Yeoman houses 7, 164-6

York 154, 155, 157, 158, 160, 163; Treasurer's House 156, 162

York, Richard, Duke of 13, 113